WordPress Styling with Blocks, Patterns, Templates, and Themes

Explore WordPress styling with step-by-step guidance, practical examples, and tips

Tammie Lister

WordPress Styling with Blocks, Patterns, Templates, and Themes

Group Product Manager: Alok Dhuri

Publishing Product Manager: Puneet Kaur

Book Project Manager: Prajakta Naik

Senior Editor: Esha Banerjee

Technical Editor: Jubit Pincy

Copy Editor: Safis Editing

Indexer: Pratik Shirodkar

Production Designer: Prafulla Nikalje

DevRel Marketing Coordinator: Deepak Kumar and Mayank Singh

First published: February 2024

Production reference: 1220224

Published by Packt Publishing Ltd.
Grosvenor House
11 St Paul's Square
Birmingham
B3 1RB, UK

ISBN 978-1-80461-850-9

www.packtpub.com

Contributors

About the author

Tammie Lister is a versatile creator with a hybrid background in psychology, coding, design, and art. She creates effective products, experiences, communities, and practices for a sustainable future. Tammie has contributed to WordPress core releases and led design for the Gutenberg editor during phase one. She got her start within the community through contribution and recognizes with thanks everyone that supported and enabled her.

Throughout her career, she has worked in various industries, with a focus on open source and startups. She has spoken, taught, and educated people worldwide on how to empower themselves by using these tools, regardless of their background.

This book couldn't have been written without the work that every contributor did to create the current state of WordPress, Blocks, Patterns, Templates, and Styling. Every single commit I would like to recognize.

I would like to call out specifically Jessica for being an incredible guide during this and for being much more than just a technical editor.

Thank you to those who have been leading knowledge and developer relations in this area; you all deserve recognition. If you have ever created a pattern or even shared a tip – thank you.

Thank you to those who have led, co-led, and been part of each release squad across the phases of the core editor, codename Gutenberg. You have all moved the project forward, including each feature, commit, line, and pixel. Thanks to those who have tested and those who have documented and written tutorials on the new things. As the project progressed, this constantly growing resource helped everyone.

To the contributors and code poets.

– Tammie Lister

About the reviewer

Jessica Lyschik is a front-end and WordPress developer at Greyd with more than 17 years of experience creating web solutions for clients of all sizes. After spending almost a decade coding with Python, she went full-time on developing for WordPress in 2015. She enjoys diving deep into creating solutions with CSS, the Block and Site Editor, and the performance optimization of WordPress websites. Jessica has been contributing to WordPress in multiple ways, most notably being the Default Theme Co-Lead for the Twenty Twenty-Four theme released with WordPress 6.4 in November 2023. She also speaks at WordCamps and other events on a regular basis.

I'd like to thank my family, friends, and the many people from the WordPress community who supported me in my journey. The WordPress community had a huge influence on my personal growth over the past decade and I'm grateful for this. Also, a special thank you to Tammie for suggesting me as technical reviewer and the team at Packt Publishing for their guidance.

Table of Contents

3

Block Styles   51

4

Blocks and Styles Wrap-Up   71

Part 2: Block Patterns

5

Understanding Block Patterns   89

6

Discovering and Creating Block Patterns   97

7

Discovering the WordPress Pattern Directory   115

8

Wrapping Up Patterns   127

Part 3: Template Parts and Templates

9

10

11

Preface

WordPress just celebrated its 20th anniversary. From its early days, this open-source project had a concept of themes that allowed styling to be packaged and customized. Later on, an entire experience for doing that customization was created. Styling content along with creating it has been at the heart because it's what someone wants to do. Creating something is amazing, but having control over how that appears without having to go and ask someone to make a small change – that's where the true power of a system like WordPress comes in.

It's been two decades with a lot of changes and even more recently with the new editing experience and potential with styling. You might have used a theme, you might have added some custom styling, or even used a plugin to customize before; now things have changed with WordPress offering built-in capabilities and opening a world of possibilities. This means you can start to create those visions in your head and truly unlock the power of WordPress to deliver your content.

In this book, we are going to learn about the available design tools and explore new editing options, including blocks and patterns. These design tools empower and make things easier that were far too complex before. Together, we will discover the site editing experience, and explore block themes, with template and template parts, along with styles.

This knowledge is going to be applied to create those designs you have in your mind without the need for extensive code. WordPress has a mission of democratizing publishing, and the recent changes in styling decorative styling – making it open to everyone who wants to do it without knowing complex code.

Who this book is for

This book is your go-to resource for exploring and unleashing your creative potential using the latest styling features available in WordPress. Whether you're a non-coder, a hobbyist, or a seasoned WordPress user, this guide will help you discover the full range of new options. With no prior knowledge assumed, each step is carefully explained to ensure that you make the most of the latest version. Starting with a no-code approach, the book progressively introduces some coding for those interested in taking their learning further.

What this book covers

Chapter 1, *Introducing Blocks*, helps us learn what a block is and what are WordPress design tools. Readers will go on to learn the history and background.

Chapter 2, *Block Design Tools*, builds on the previous chapter, taking the knowledge of the design tools and moving into understanding each category.

Chapter 3, Block Styles, explores what block styles are and how to use the existing ones.

Chapter 4, Block and Styles Wrap-Up, concludes our section on blocks and ends with combining everything we have learned so far. It will include the design tools and also provide some tips along the way.

Chapter 5, Understanding Block Patterns, begins our journey with patterns. It will take the reader by the hand and begin by sharing what patterns are and their power.

Chapter 6, Discovering and Creating Block Patterns, guides the reader through discovering how to create patterns and then share them. It is a very practical chapter focused on walking through each step.

Chapter 7, Discovering the WordPress Pattern Directory, focuses on the WordPress Pattern Directory, which is a free resource of patterns, available for anyone. The reader will learn how to find a pattern, add it to their content, and be able to use it. This chapter will unlock a world of possibilities for them.

Chapter 8, Wrapping Up Patterns, ends the journey around patterns and looks to inspire with some creative ones. Looking beyond simple patterns and how even they might be art, it encourages the reader to explore and unleash their creativity.

Chapter 9, An Introduction to Site Editing, takes the reader through the concept of WordPress site editing. This introduction itself should inspire the reader to create their own templates.

Chapter 10, Discovering and Creating Template Parts, takes the reader through understanding what template parts are and how they are different from templates. They will be able to learn how to use them fully.

Chapter 11, Discovering and Creating Templates, talks about what templates are and how to use them in the editor and full site editing experience. Through examples, they will be guided and shown how to use, edit, and manage.

Chapter 12, Templates Wrap-Up, delves a little more into how you can, by knowing the template hierarchy, unlock some pretty cool aspects of templates, from creating one just for single posts to truly custom experiences.

Chapter 13, Understanding How Themes Have Changed, takes the reader through a brief history to understand why themes have changed and how we got here, and why. It also shared some inspiring samples.

Chapter 14, Discovering Styles, delves into styles and why, in the recent times, they are central to WordPress styling and themes. They unlock powerful styling for which you would need to know CSS beforehand.

Chapter 15, Discovering WordPress Block Themes, explores the concept called block themes and what this means. From there, they will learn how to use and find these new themes – truly unlock their power to take advantage of all the new styling possibilities.

Chapter 16, Wrapping Up Themes, closes the book, and the topic of themes will be wrapped up – showing the reader how inspiring themes can be. This will leave the reader hopeful for the future of WordPress styling, excited and optimistic about all the possibilities.

To get the most out of this book

Readers will discover WordPress styling is far more than just themes, and the entire world from blocks, patterns, and templates – will open up and empower them all without having to know code. Learn how to use these features together as they build up to create WordPress your way truly.

Historically people felt they needed to know code to style WordPress, from CSS to even more. This is no longer the case, and incredible tools are built in. However, discovering those is hard; this book uncovers and supports them and guides you to unleash your creativity.

You need to have WordPress installed for trying out the learnings from this book.

If you are using the digital version of this book, we advise you to type the code yourself or access the code from the book's GitHub repository (a link is available in the next section). Doing so will help you avoid any potential errors related to the copying and pasting of code.

Download the example code files

You can download the example code files for this book from GitHub at `https://github.com/PacktPublishing/WordPress-styling-with-blocks-patterns-templates-and-themes-`. If there's an update to the code, it will be updated in the GitHub repository.

We also have other code bundles from our rich catalog of books and videos available at `https://github.com/PacktPublishing/`. Check them out!

Download the color images

The color images in this book can be viewed at `https://packt.link/gbp/9781804618509`.

Conventions used

There are a number of text conventions used throughout this book.

`Code in text`: Indicates code words in text, database table names, folder names, filenames, file extensions, pathnames, dummy URLs, user input, and Twitter handles. Here is an example: " If you want to do this via JavaScript you can use a similar path using the `unregister_block_style` function."

A block of code is set as follows:

```
function prefix_remove_core_block_styles() {

wp_dequeue_style( 'wp-block-quote' );

}

add_action( 'wp_enqueue_scripts', 'prefix_remove_core_block_styles' );
[default]
```

Bold: Indicates a new term, an important word, or words that you see onscreen. For instance, words in menus or dialog boxes appear in **bold**. Here is an example: " This editor can be found under **Appearance** by selecting **Editor**, as you can see in *Figure 9.1*."

> **Tips or important notes**
> Appear like this.

Get in touch

Feedback from our readers is always welcome.

General feedback: If you have questions about any aspect of this book, email us at customercare@packtpub.com and mention the book title in the subject of your message.

Errata: Although we have taken every care to ensure the accuracy of our content, mistakes do happen. If you have found a mistake in this book, we would be grateful if you would report this to us. Please visit www.packtpub.com/support/errata and fill in the form.

Piracy: If you come across any illegal copies of our works in any form on the internet, we would be grateful if you would provide us with the location address or website name. Please contact us at copyright@packt.com with a link to the material.

If you are interested in becoming an author: If there is a topic that you have expertise in and you are interested in either writing or contributing to a book, please visit authors.packtpub.com.

Share Your Thoughts

Once you've read *WordPress Styling with Blocks, Patterns, Templates and Themes*, we'd love to hear your thoughts! Scan the QR code below to go straight to the Amazon review page for this book and share your feedback.

https://packt.link/r/1804618500

Your review is important to us and the tech community and will help us make sure we're delivering excellent quality content.

Download a free PDF copy of this book

Thanks for purchasing this book!

Do you like to read on the go but are unable to carry your print books everywhere?

Is your e-book purchase not compatible with the device of your choice?

Don't worry!, Now with every Packt book, you get a DRM-free PDF version of that book at no cost.

Read anywhere, any place, on any device. Search, copy, and paste code from your favorite technical books directly into your application.

The perks don't stop there, you can get exclusive access to discounts, newsletters, and great free content in your inbox daily

Follow these simple steps to get the benefits:

1. Scan the QR code or visit the following link:

https://packt.link/free-ebook/9781804618509

2. Submit your proof of purchase.
3. That's it! We'll send your free PDF and other benefits to your email directly.

Part 1: Styling and Design Tools

Blocks are the foundation of the WordPress editor. In this part, you will discover what is a block, how to style it, and what is a design tool.

This section has the following chapters:

- *Chapter 1, Introducing Blocks*
- *Chapter 2, Block Design Tools*
- *Chapter 3, Block Styles*
- *Chapter 4, Block and Styles Wrap-up*

1
Introducing Blocks

Our main objective in this book is to learn about the new editing experience in WordPress, which was code-named Gutenberg, and find out how to style with a **block-based editor**. This starts with understanding the concepts of block-based editors. In order to set up the work to be done in this book, we will explore what setup you will need and also how default themes work. We'll then move on to creating styling that was previously hard to achieve. We do this by discovering design tools. In this chapter, we will cover the following topics:

- A new way of creating
- Discovering WordPress
- What is a block?
- What are design tools?
- Key concepts

By the end of this chapter, you will be able to add blocks and find whatever block you want, use the editor, and know how to add simple design tools.

A new way of creating

Before the changes to the editor in WordPress, creating and editing content was done using a simpler format with limited functionality. This editor, often referred to as the "Classic Editor," while easy to use, was not very flexible and often made it difficult to create complex layouts and designs without using code or plugins. Often people would have to learn frameworks and systems to get simple tasks done, which on other platforms would be built-in. This meant that, for anything complicated, you would have to either learn coding or hire someone to assist you.

The world outside WordPress was starting to use block-based interfaces you could drag and drop, putting content at the heart of creating and empowering users through built-in tools. A decision was made that, to compete, the editor needed to change. This project was called Gutenberg, after Johannes Gutenberg, the printing press inventor, who revolutionized how information was shared and distributed.

> **Note**
> Gutenberg for WordPress was first introduced as a plugin in 2017 and later released into the product core in 2018 with WordPress 5.0.

This new editor made it possible to create much more complex and dynamic layouts and allowed users to interact with content blocks and styles without knowing the code.

There are several phases of this WordPress project, called Gutenberg, and so far, two have been completed: *easier editing* and *customization*. The current phase of the project is collaboration, and then multilingual.

It wasn't just the interface that changed, though. The system of using blocks to create content, and the manner in which this was done, brought about a change in styling opportunities that were also drastically different. This allowed the creation of rich content that was flexible and available to a whole new range of people who were previously unable to use it due to the need for custom code or plugins. Here, as you can see in *Figure 1.1*, we have the editor itself. This is also known as the **Block Editor** when you are using blocks to create your site, not editing your entire site – where it would be referred to as the **Site Editor**.

Figure 1.1 – WordPress Block Editor

The Block Editor has paved an entirely new way to create and style content within WordPress. Previously, where you needed to code, you can now add a block and style using design tools. This has been a foundational change in how things are created within WordPress.

Have you ever wanted to change something such as a font family or even something fancy, such as implementing some incredible duotone effect you've seen on images online? Previously, you'd have to do this using custom CSS or a plugin. This meant it was often inaccessible to many, yet it formed the basics of content creation – controlling simple styling.

One of the foundations of the work done in the first phase of the new editor was to bring the possibility of styling to more people. To do this, it had to go back to basics; it needed to start with the most simple format, that is, starting with blocks.

> **Note**
>
> If you are creating a new WordPress install, you most likely will have Twenty Twenty-Four activated by default at the time of this being published. What theme you use is up to you.
>
> Throughout this book, we are going to be using default themes and alternating different ones all the way back to Twenty Twenty-Two. It's useful to get to explore and know different ones, so as you walk through the examples, take time to get to know each theme also.

Discovering WordPress

In this book, there are many opportunities to follow along with examples. You can do that using your own site, often referred to as a local install or a demo site:

- **Use WordPress Playground**: This enables you to have a demo site, but is just in the browser, so anything you create will be removed each time. You can start trying this right here: `https://wordpress.org/playground/`.

- **Install locally**: This means having a server on your own computer you can use. There is a helpful guide on this within the WordPress handbook: `https://make.wordpress.org/core/handbook/tutorials/installing-a-local-server/`.

- **Use hosting**: You can have a website on a host and use file transfer, often even editing files through a hosting dashboard. Many hosts have "one-click" WordPress installs that make this easy for you too.

What is a block?

Blocks are the smallest unit of content and when combined they form the content or layout of a webpage. These blocks can contain text, images, videos, buttons, and many more types of content.

You can combine these blocks to create the structure and shape of your site, the same way you used building blocks as a child to play and build a variety of things. Within the editing interface, blocks can be added, removed, and rearranged using drag-and-drop or keyboard interactions.

They are a flexible and intuitive way to create content in WordPress without using any code. Blocks already come in the editor, but you can create your own with some coding or get them from the WordPress plugin directory.

Whatever you can think of – there is a block for that!

Discovering blocks in the editor

Finding blocks is done in several different ways; first, start typing. That's it … you've found your first block – the **paragraph** one. See *Figure 1.2*. Here, you can see the paragraph block added to the editor.

Figure 1.2 – The paragraph block

Want a header? Let's do that together and show two methods of finding blocks.

Click the + icon, as shown in *Figure 1.3*, to browse whatever block you want and click and add it. The + icon is also known as the plus icon and enables you to add things to your content. It will appear in different places, as we will discover together now.

Figure 1.3 – Selecting a block from the block inserter

Here, in *Figure 1.3*, you can see the + icon appending blocks within the content. This appears just like the one in the toolbar to help you add content. You can also click **Browse all** to see the block library in its complete form, and even previews. See *Figure 1.4*.

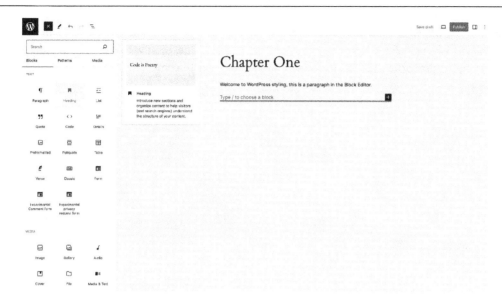

Figure 1.4 – Browsing the full block library panel

Click the block you want to add, and there you go.

Adding blocks faster

The / (forward slash) command is another easy way to add blocks. It allows you to quickly get the blocks added while you are in the flow of adding. In the following screenshot, you can see what you get when clicking /.

Figure 1.5 – Using / to add blocks

At times when you wish to focus on your writing, you can use the fullscreen mode (see *Figure 1.5*). This typically is your default view when first editing. In this mode, even with the sidebar visible to show the block's properties, you get to use all the space on your screen.

Figure 1.6 – Selecting fullscreen mode

> **Note**
>
> Under modes, you can adjust a range of options for your views. This way, you can customize your editing experience to how you want it. There is even **Spotlight mode**! Look at *Figure 1.6*. Using **Spotlight mode** and **Distraction free**, you can create an experience as shown in *Figure 1.7*. Have you ever wanted to see the outline of your content when in the editor? This handy little tip will allow you to do just that. Click **Document overview**, the stacked line icon, in the toolbar, and the following screen (*Figure 1.7*) opens; you can then navigate around it.

There is a lot you can do in this view, from grouping blocks to navigation and reordering.

Figure 1.7 – List view within the editor

Want to know things such as stats – how much you've written, for example? No problem. Click the second tab, called **Outline**, as shown in *Figure 1.8*. You can also see useful heading structures, which really help SEO and accessibility.

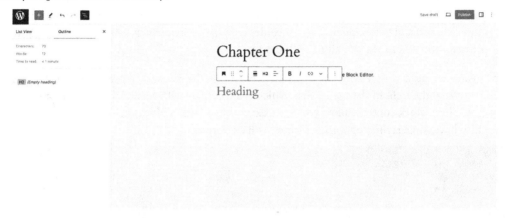

Figure 1.8 – The Outline tab

Blocks have several essential functions they all share. These can be found under block settings within the block toolbar. Let's look into each block setting, one by one, as numbered in *Figure 1.9*.

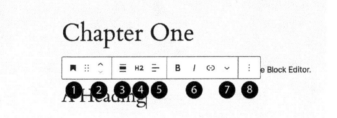

Figure 1.9 – Block settings

1. **Block label**: What appears here depends on the theme and block. From quick transform to changing types, styles and patterns – you can access a range of helpful options.

2. **Movers and drag handles**: This gives you the ability to grab the block to drag it up and down. Using the arrows is a way to click to reorder.

3. **Alignment**: This is for the block itself.

4. **Block-specific controls**: Here, headings can be changed to other heading levels (H1, H3, H4).

5. **Text alignment**: This is for those blocks that are text.

6. **Text styling**: Anything that adds styling to text, for example bold, italic, and linking.

7. **Additional tools**: There is a dropdown that offers additional tools such as the use of footnotes, highlights, inline code, inline images, keyboard input, language, strikethrough, and sub and superscript. This opens the extra menus for text styling.

8. **More options**: This is where you get block-specific controls for all blocks, for example, copy, duplicate, and add before/after. It also includes copy/paste styles, lock, rename, create pattern, move to, and edit as HTML, along with delete.

There is also a secondary place where you can find controls in the sidebar. To get there, you click the second icon from the right in the top toolbar, which is a rectangle with a smaller one to the side. See *Figure 1.10*. These block controls allow you to do extra things with a block that might be specific to it. They also have some styling options, which we will explore later.

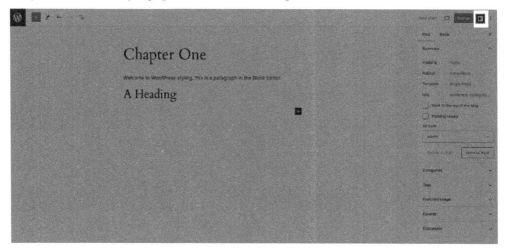

Figure 1.10 – Secondary block controls

Moving a block is easy; you use the movers. You must have selected the block to see these, with the keyboard or mouse.

In *Figure 1.11*, you can see there are arrows within the toolbar. These can be used to move the block and are called the block movers.

Figure 1.11 – Showing the block movers and the selection of a block

This isn't the only way to move a block. *Figure 1.12* shows using the "more" menu to move a block by selecting **Move to**. This is another option when looking to order your content.

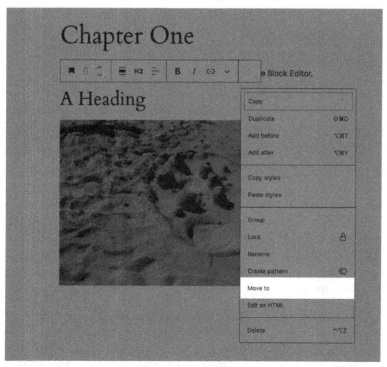

Figure 1.12 – Selecting and moving a block

As well as the arrows shown in the toolbar and the **Move to** option, there are even more ways to move blocks. You can move them using **List View**, which allows you to move them while seeing the entire overview. This can be found under **Document Overview**.

Now that we know what a block is, let's find out what we can do with them by exploring the design tools.

Reset values

Within the editor, there is always the option to undo and redo; this is great as a step-by-step method of going back and forward. You can access that at the top of the editing screen, as shown in *Figure 1.13*.

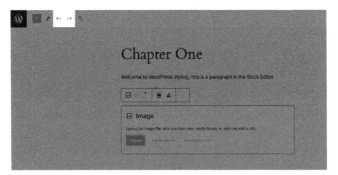

Figure 1.13 – Undo and redo controls

What are design tools?

Design tools is a term for anything relating to the appearance of blocks. WordPress has an "everything is a block" concept, meaning all content. This translates to design tools impacting all of your content's appearance. These tools cover everything from *colors*, *typography*, *alignments*, and *positioning* to *filters* and *cropping*. It's a simple interface to apply styles.

At the start, things were very different in WordPress if you wanted to style content. Often, it was hard, as we have learned, and you either needed to know how to code, know someone who could code, or know the "ways" of WordPress. This has changed fundamentally with the new editing experience and design tools. Historically, if you wanted to go down the non-code route for styling, you could look away from the core WordPress product and consider a framework, or perhaps even a stack of plugins and a complicated theme system. It wasn't something that could be taken lightly and often meant you couldn't easily change things if you wanted to later – for example, freshening up your theme or even updating WordPress rapidly becoming more complex.

One of the ways in which easier styling has been achieved is by setting boundaries to style within. This means you can experiment, grow, and flourish as you style. Your site won't crash or cause conflicts or problematic situations you need to debug. Due to being supported by the system you are working on, within the core, the interface works no matter what design tool you use. Developers can provide options even in the themes and plugins they create that use these styling boundaries.

Design tools level the ground, providing everyone with a base to build on. They bring an interface you know you can come to trust as each tool uses the same principles. For example, you can learn about font sizing, using the same interface no matter the block. The same applies to each design tool, from color picking and duotone to gradients and more.

> **Note**
>
> These tools can also be set within the theme by the creator, so what you see might depend on the theme you are using.

In this chapter, we are using Twenty Twenty-Four (https://wordpress.org/themes/twentytwentyfour/) which has design tools active as shown in *Figure 1.14*.

Figure 1.14 – Editor side panel showing design tools

The preceding screenshot shows how you can combine design tools to create powerful combinations, for example, using a solid color opacity on a duotone set on a cover block image background.

Imagine this: you want to change the border radius of a button block. Before blocks, there was no button block, and before design tools, you couldn't easily do this. Now, you can simply click those options under the **Styles** tab and jump into them. See *Figure 1.14*.

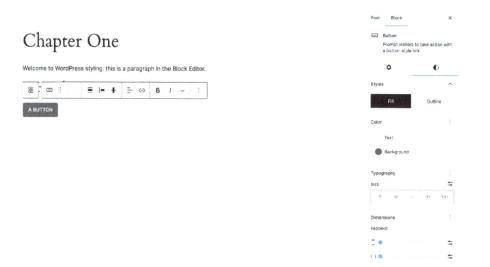

Figure 1.15 – Editor side panel showing design tools for a button

The styling options can be simple or incredibly complex; for example, with the fancy styling of the duotone filter of the image block as shown in *Figure 1.16*.

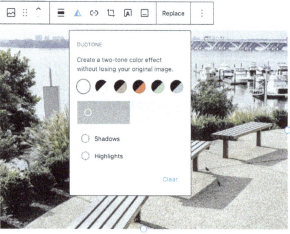

Figure 1.16 – Duotone options under block settings

By providing these design tools that people know they can trust and rely on, people can be empowered to create. The tools are baked into the system, iterated, and predictable. Since the same tools and interface are used, we can easily rely on them. This was one of the past issues with WordPress, where styling often meant learning about multiple interfaces.

Design tools solve this problem, by providing an interface for tools, which was previously accessible only in code. Powerful options are in the hands of creators of all levels. With regard to options, you will find a fine balance – neither too many nor too few.

One key part of these tools is they can be combined across blocks with patterns, but we will cover that later. They are also growing in the blocks they support and becoming increasingly unified, so what is covered here might change, but reflects the current state of WordPress.

The challenge of using these design tools is balancing giving you the styling you want without getting in the way of the theme you are using or what you want to view your site on.

Types of design tools

Design tools contain a wealth of features. They also have common categories across blocks:

- **Typography**: font size/weight/family, for example, but much more
- **Dimensions and spacing, padding, margins**, and so much more
- **Colors**: text, background, and even fantastic things such as duotone features
- **Layout**: only applying to content blocks such as buttons, columns, and gallery – impact the layout of blocks with these
- **Border**: radius, color, and even style
- **Shadows**: a feature since WordPress 6.2

In *Chapter 2*, we will go into each of these in more detail.

Key concepts

It's useful to call out a few key concepts around the design tools as we wrap up this chapter and dig deeper into each of them.

Block first

By their nature, they are "block first." They are attached to the blocks themselves, either exposed within the toolbar as in the case of duotone or through the side panel as in the case of other options such as margin and padding.

If you combine blocks into a group, you can apply the design tools to that block. This is a powerful way to build up applying styles. Hence, everything starts with the block, and that includes design tools and your content.

Intrinsic web design

One of the first questions you may ask while exploring more is where are the responsive controls within the design tools?

There are none within the editor today. While this doesn't mean there won't be at some point, they'll have to – like all tools – be the right ones. The editor is built on intrinsic web design principles. This means that it works irrespective of screen size. The layout adapts and doesn't add the complexity of trying to work out how to handle things across patterns or blocks. Intrinsic web design is a website design approach that focuses on creating flexible and adaptable layouts.

What does the term **intrinsic web design** mean though?

Well, it was coined in 2018 by *Jen Simmons* in her presentation titled *Everything You Know About Web Design Just Changed*. In simple terms, she talks about true responsiveness, flexibility, and adaptability that is true to the nature of the web. This includes using all the new features, at the time, of CSS, to create an experience that works no matter what you are viewing it on.

What does that mean for you, using the WordPress editor today?

The reality is there are enormous amounts of screen sizes now and supporting every single point, fixing content to those is not getting any easier. There will often be a time when using points where the styling looks bad as you stagger up and down in size.

Intrinsic in the editor means your content is created from the block to look good no matter what device it is viewed on, to be truly adaptable. There are also design tools that exist today, such as typography and layout tools, to help you keep to this concept without having to know anything else or set each breakpoint. This avoids missing one of the so many screen sizes and variations that exist today.

Interface not code

A rather obvious concept is adding an interface to many things for which previously you would have needed to know how to code. This means that the editor not only provides an interface but also allows us to use the same styling options for the same thing across tools. For example, let's look at range controls. These are controls that allow you to set styling, typically with a slider between a range of options. See *Figure 1.17*.

Figure 1.17 – Editor side panel showing range controls on button block.

This quote from the *Block Editor Handbook* explains some of the key interface concepts.

> *Blocks come in many different forms but also provide a consistent interface. They can be inserted, moved, reordered, copied, duplicated, transformed, deleted, dragged, and combined. Blocks can also be reused, allowing them to be shared across posts and post types and/or used multiple times in the same post. If it helps, you can think of blocks as a more graceful shortcode, with rich formatting tools for users to compose content.*

```
https://developer.wordpress.org/block-editor/explanations/architecture/
key-concepts/
```

The interface empowers you, as you can learn how to do something once, and then you can do it across any block that has that tool or setting in the future. For example, once you learn how to change the size of a font, move a block, or even set borders and background colors, it's the same for all blocks going forward using the design tools in WordPress.

Summary

We are just starting our adventure together discovering WordPress styling. Today, you can create far more than what was previously possible. In this chapter, we have learned a lot together. So, let's go through what we have covered:

- Gutenberg is the code name for a new editing experience in WordPress. This has opened up the opportunity to do things for which previously you needed to understand code.

- Today's content in WordPress is built up using blocks of different types, from images to text, with unique blocks such as the cover block and traditional ones such as headings.

- We learned that blocks have settings that we can access through primary and secondary areas.

- Also, we learned how to set the mode and style of our editing experience, along with the outline, and see the details of the content we are creating.

- WordPress has a concept of design tools, which are tools to empower styling. Further, we learned that there are concepts that all design tools use.

- Finally, we familiarized ourselves with the different types of design tools, which are color, layout, border, and shadow.

This is all great, but design tools have a lot more to them. In the next chapter, we will look at each of these and even see how you can combine them powerfully to create incredible style combinations.

Questions

Answer the following questions to test your knowledge of this chapter:

1. Please select the false statement

   a. The code name for the block-based editor of WordPress is Gutenberg.

   b. The code name for the block-based editor of WordPress is Blockberg.

2. Movers for blocks can be found:

   a. By the block in the block toolbar.

   b. In the settings sidebar.

3. Which new feature came out in 6.2 for design tools?

   a. Typography

   b. Dimensions

   c. Shadows

4.   Define a block.

a. Blocks are the smallest unit of content and when combined they form the content or layout of a webpage.

b. WordPress blocks are a brand new plugin that is a page builder.

c. WordPress blocks are limited units of content that can only be ordered in a set way to create pages and posts on a WordPress website.

Answers

1.   Please select the false statement

b. The code name for the block-based editor of WordPress is Blockberg.

2.   Movers for blocks can be found:

a. By the block in the block toolbar.

3.   Which new feature came out in 6.2 for design tools?

c. Shadows

4.   Define a block.

a. Blocks are the smallest unit of content and when combined they form the content or layout of a webpage.

Further reading

To learn more about the topics that were covered in this chapter, take a look at the following resources:

- *Block Editor Handbook*: https://developer.wordpress.org/block-editor/
- *The Ship of Theseus, changing the editor*: https://matiasventura.com/post/gutenberg-or-the-ship-of-theseus/
- *Release of Gutenberg, the Block Editor in WordPress 5.0*: https://wordpress.org/news/2018/12/bebo/
- *Hidden features of the editor*: https://gutenbergtimes.com/the-secret-manual-hidden-features-wordpress-gutenberg/
- *Jen Simmon's Intrinsic Web Design Lab*: https://labs.jensimmons.com/

2

Block Design Tools

This chapter goes a little further into design tools, exploring each of them and the types of tools offered. Design tools are useful to style blocks and elevate your designs, unlocking capabilities that previously required you to know how to code. So, together, we will go through examples and look at how you can use these tools.

In this chapter, we will go over the following:

- Stepping into design tools
- Typography
- Dimensions and spacing
- Color
- Layout
- Borders
- Shadows
- Leveling up design tools

Stepping into design tools

In the previous chapter, we learned about the different types of design tools and how they can be helpful in unlocking the power of complex design combinations. We also discussed how their simple interfaces make them accessible to anyone. In this chapter, we will delve into each type of tool and learn how to use their interfaces to unlock their full capabilities for ourselves.

It's worth noting that some design tools are experimental. So, when you want to use them in your own theme, always check whether it has the "experimental" flag. Carefully consider implementing those tools in your code and evaluate whether to use them or not.

Variations in design tools

As we embark on our exploration of design tools, it's important to note that the appearance and functionality of these tools can differ based on various factors. Firstly, the theme being used can affect the availability of tools and their default values, which can be set in a file called `theme.json`. We will delve into this further in the chapter on global styling (*Chapter 14*), specifically in the last sections of the book when we discuss block themes.

Secondly, the editor where you access these tools can also impact the number of options and blocks available. In a later chapter, we will delve into this topic and the associated tools. For now, this chapter will focus on the tools available when creating content, such as a page or post.

Using design tools

In this section, we are going to cover an overview of what design tools are. Then, we are going to look at the **Image** and **Gallery** blocks as examples of how to use them.

To begin using design tools, let's explore how to find them. Luckily, there are two places to locate these tools. The first can be found within the block itself, such as the **Image** block, which includes the duotone tools in the block toolbar. See *Figure 2.1*. This is quite a simple process.

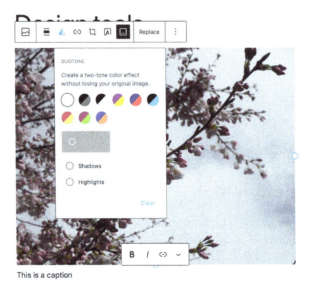

This is a caption

Figure 2.1 – Image block with duotone tools

Some blocks have their tools in the settings sidebar. In these next examples, we are using the theme Twenty Twenty-Three. You can access this by clicking the block itself. The settings sidebar should then open automatically, as shown in *Figure 2.2*.

Figure 2.2 – Image block showing design tools in the settings sidebar

Let's explore the **Gallery** block, which contains a variety of tools. These tools can be found in the **Block** section, located in the settings sidebar. However, there's a specific toolbar for block settings that we'll also be directed to. It's a really cool feature; let's head there now. We get there by selecting a **Gallery** block and adding some images to it. Then we click on the toolbar. Once you have done that, you will see what is shown in *Figure 2.3*.

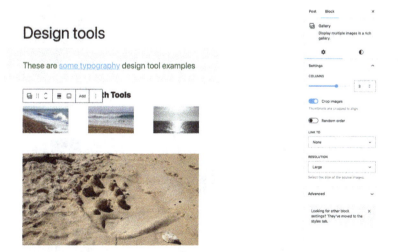

Figure 2.3 – Showing the block settings sidebar with the message redirecting you

Select the styles tab, which is the icon shown in the following screenshot. With this, you can access those tools for the selected block, which in *Figure 2.3* is the **Gallery** block. Here you can see the tools provided, and you can then focus on creating the perfect design using those tools.

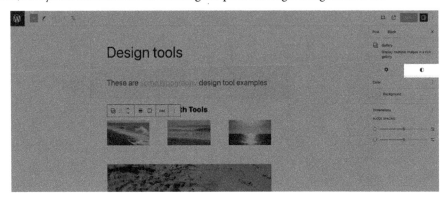

Figure 2.4 – Gallery block settings

Independent tools

If a design tool has multiple directional options, for example, a border or spacing at the top, bottom, left and right – it is also possible to "unlink" these options. In *Figure 2.5*, you can see the tool in context, allowing you to set borders on the **Gallery** block we were using before.

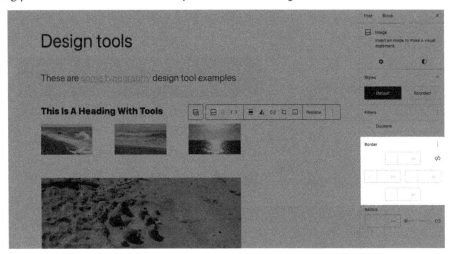

Figure 2.5 – Unlinked border settings

This is useful to get that precise control as you explore and dive deeper with design tools, allowing you to create things your way.

Resetting design tools

When using these design tools, it is important to have the ability to reset. There may be times when you want to undo something, but using the undo button within the editor may not be sufficient. In such cases, you can reset either specific values or everything at once. For instance, in *Figure 2.6*, you can reset just the link color, or reset all colors simultaneously.

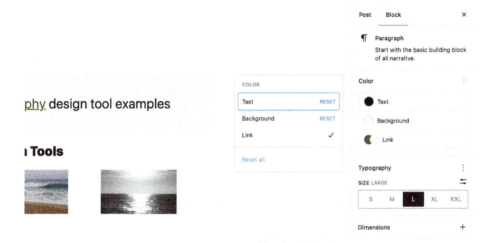

Figure 2.6 – Reset tool: RESET and Reset all options

Sometimes, you may want to be able to go back, and while you always have those options at the top of the editing interface with undo and redo, you can also use these settings for greater control.

Custom values

Most design tools have different options; you can change them to create different combinations. To set a custom value, as in the case here in the **Gallery** block, you can click the icon shown in *Figure 2.7*, which opens up an interface to set a custom value.

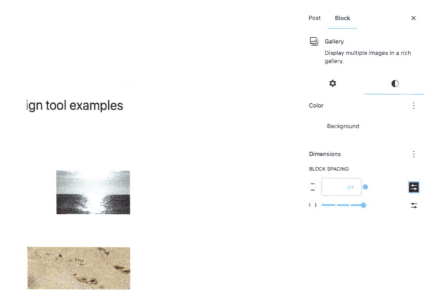

Figure 2.7 – Icon to show custom values

You can do this for a range, including those with typography design tools to set specific values and units such as px or em. This gives you the granular control you need over your design.

Let's now move on and see what we can do with typography.

Typography

Typography relies heavily on fundamental design tools such as font size, style, weight, line height, text transformation, and decoration. By skillfully combining these settings, you can create impressive typography. It's essential to note that the typography you can use depends on the theme's settings.

For example, if your theme only has one font family, you will be limited to that family. Keep in mind that when using block design tools in the editor, you are working within certain limits. There will be a font library feature bringing easier font management. At the time of writing, this is listed for WordPress 6.5 around March 2024.

For most themes, the **Paragraph** block is the simplest interface for typography. Here, as you can see in *Figure 2.8*, you can find the size value and access basic formatting tools such as bold, italic, underline, and strikethrough through the toolbar by clicking the down arrow. The sidebar also has some simple settings that depend on the theme. The design tools you see depend on what is available within the theme, what defaults are turned on, and what is set.

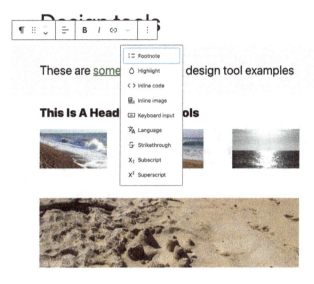

Figure 2.8 – Paragraph block showing toolbar settings

Let's start by looking at a standard interface for the **Heading** block:

1. Add a **Heading** block to your page. Type whatever you want to get started. In this example, I am using the Twenty Twenty-Three default WordPress theme. Make sure you use it if you're following along to have the same styles.

2. Select the block and see what options are available here with the settings sidebar showing.

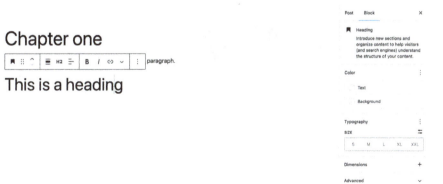

Figure 2.9 – Heading block with settings

3. You can see the typography tools available for the **Heading** block. Let's start simply by increasing the heading size to **XXL**. Just click that option and you should see it change.

Figure 2.10 – Changing the font size on the Heading block

4. Great! Let's do something else; what about changing **APPEARANCE** to **Black**?

Figure 2.11 – Changing the appearance on the Heading block

5. Now, to finish up, let's change the letter case by selecting the capitalize option, as shown in *Figure 2.12*.

6. Don't forget to save and preview your work, and then publish. It might not always autosave, and losing the work you've done so far would be a shame. It also won't save everything until you select **Publish**.

Figure 2.12 – Setting capitalization on Heading block

How cool is that? All this was done without having to change a line of code.

By combining your theme's settings, even block by block, you can scale up and unlock some incredible typography. We are now going to explore some interesting typography options.

Blocks available

There are typography design tools that can be used for any block that contains text, ranging from paragraphs and headings to lists and **Cover** blocks. Even button blocks can be customized with typography using simple selection methods. Various blocks, such as verse, quote, site tagline, and button, include text, and many themes incorporate unique styling with these blocks. As you can see in *Figure 2.13*, **Typography** settings can also be selected within the **Paragraph** block.

Figure 2.13 – Adding a typography value

You can also change the typography; let's do that now!

1. Add a **Heading** block.

2. Let's change the **Typography** scale to **px**. By default, typography is in predefined sizes (**S**, **M**, **L**, **XL**, and **XXL**) but this depends on the theme. To change this, select the icon above the size scale that has two lines and two dots. Once you click this, you have the option to add a custom value, and can add one outside those predefined.

Clicking on "**px**" allows you to change the type of units and which is default will depend on your theme. In our case let's add 29px into the custom field, as shown in *Figure 2.14*.

Figure 2.14 – Custom typography value

Using these custom value controls lets you quickly get that finite control over typography that takes your design to the next level.

Dimensions and spacing

This toolset includes padding, margin, block gap, height, width, and min size – all enabling control over the layout of blocks compared to inner or nearby blocks. An excellent example of this would be how the **Gallery** block works. For this example, let's use the theme Twenty Twenty-Four.

Let's begin exploring dimensions and spacing by adding a **Gallery** block:

1. Add a **Gallery** block with three images. You can then change the layout using the **COLUMNS** setting, as seen here to be 2 columns. See *Figure 2.15*.

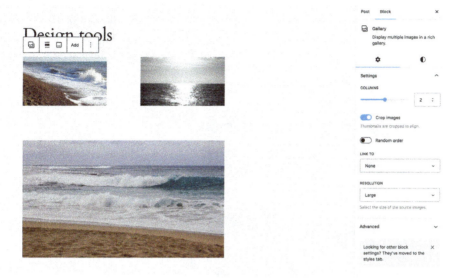

Figure 2.15 – Adjusting columns in the Gallery block

2. Something to consider with galleries is that they contain individual blocks – and that's where spacing comes in with the gaps between. If you go to the styling tools (see *Figure 2.15*; remember, you can get to the styles tab by clicking the circle that is half filled), you can see the **BLOCK SPACING** setting and the option to change it. Let's increase it a little to give some more space.

Figure 2.16 – Adjusting spacing in dimensions

3.   Notice the three-dot icon beside **Dimensions**; this provides more options for settings. Let's click this and see what else we have available. By default, depending on your theme, different options will be set. For example, here, the margin and spacing are turned off by default.

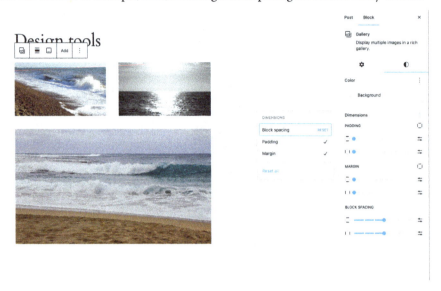

Figure 2.17 – Showing the adjusted spacing in dimensions

Once you enable them, you have them available as controls, giving you even more potential.

Color

The color design tools provide a range of options, including text, background, links, gradients, and duotone filters. These tools are incredibly versatile and available in almost every block depending on their capabilities.

With the text tool, you can easily change the color of your text. The background tool allows you to choose the background color of your blocks. The color of the links tool is also available, and hover state is now supported in some themes.

Various blocks, such as **Columns**, **Gallery**, **Social Links**, **Code**, and **Calendar**, support these features, allowing you to add more color to your content. You can even add color to links, which can be seen in *Figure 2.18*.

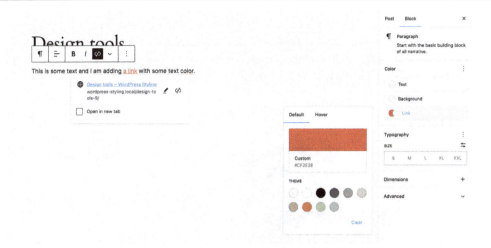

Figure 2.18 – Link color

You can explore more link styling within the Site Editor, where you get even more control over the states of links, for example, within the **Navigation** block. We are going to come back to this block over the course of the book, learning more about it as we go, including a more in-depth walk-through.

There is a handy little tool built into the design tools that checks the accessibility. Let's test this now. In *Figure 2.19*, you can see I picked a color that doesn't meet the standards. The contrast ratio being used is 4.5:1.

Figure 2.19 – Accessibility color message

This message lets you know that the contrast may be hard for people to read and advises on how you can improve accessibility.

Beyond simple colors

There is so much more to design tools than colors; what about gradients? Let's add one to a cover image – how cool would that be? Cover images don't just have to be images; you can use color and create a fantastic gradient design:

1. Add a cover image to a new post or page. As shown in *Figure 2.20*, select the setting under COLOR. Then, select the block within the style tab. Ensure you have Overlay selected and then select Gradient, next to Solid. Once you add a new cover block, the block should be selected and this tab should be open for you.

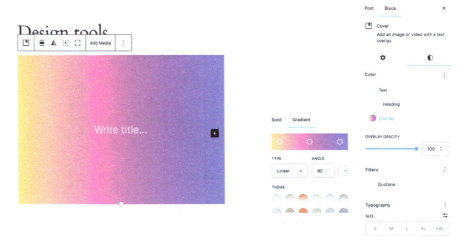

Figure 2.20 – Gradient control

2. Let's pick a gradient preset from the list here. What we have already looks good for a cover. How about mixing things up, though? Let's change the type to **Radial**. See *Figure 2.21*.

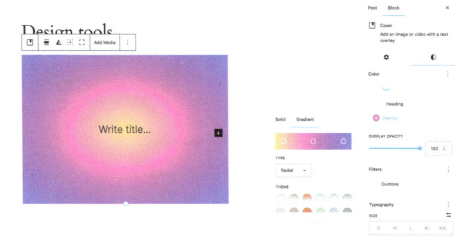

Figure 2.21 – Radial gradient

3. You can see how to create exciting options using different combinations. You can also combine the overlay opacity with solid backgrounds to explore exciting combinations.

> **Note**
> Gradients, duotones, or colors can, depending on the theme functionality, either be disabled or limited to those determined within the theme. If the theme allows it, you can click on any color shown on the white circle within the editor and it will open a color picker, allowing you to mix any combination of colors your heart desires.

So far, we've just been showing some specific tools around coloring, but there is also an exciting tool called duotone. Duotone can be accessed both from the block toolbar and the settings sidebar. This has a range of presets, which can be set within the theme. It applies to any image; you can see it applied to one here, in *Figure 2.22*.

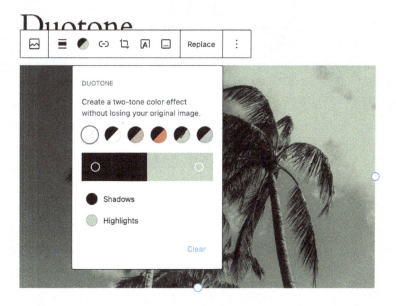

Figure 2.22 – Using duotone

Now, just applying this is excellent, but duotone can serve various purposes. What about using it to turn a color image into a black-and-white image? Let's do that now:

Pick an Image block and select an image from your media library.

Figure 2.23 – Image block

Click the duotone option in the toolbar – remember that you may find some other design tools there depending on the block selected. Note in the screenshot you can also see there is the option in the design tools side panel to access duotone.

The duotone icon is the triangle that changes to a circle when active it, as shown in *Figure 2.24*. Now select the grayscale option, and this will instantly remove the color from your image.

Figure 2.24 – Grayscale on an Image block

This is a fantastic way of creating a unified look for images. You can also do this by applying, of course, the same duotone; many themes have their own presets you can use for this.

That finishes our exploration of colors. Now let's move on to looking at **Layout**.

Layout

This tool is more advanced and is used for adjusting the layout of content blocks such as buttons, columns, and galleries. It specifically affects the arrangement of blocks within each other. Some examples of blocks that can be affected are comments, queries, posts, social links, and post content, and templates.

Navigation blocks can be a complex example to understand, but it is important to consider them in the overall editing context. The **Layout** tool is powerful and controls complex blocks. To see how it works, let's examine how it affects a **Columns** block.

Add a **Columns** block with two columns, then put some paragraph text in one column and an image in the other. Then, click on the first column to see the following layout options. In order to get to the first column, you have two options: either click on the **Paragraph** block and select the first icon in the block toolbar to go up one level to the column or use the list view from the top toolbar to select the first column in the **Columns** block.

As shown in *Figure 2.25*, you can turn "on" **Inner blocks use content width**, and you should see a range of options. You will notice the following message `Nested blocks will fill the width of this container for full and wide widths`.

Figure 2.25 – Layout controls for columns

In this interface, you have more control over the width, justification, and other advanced settings compared to other design tools. However, the availability of these options depends on the selected theme. By default, these settings may not be visible. In simpler terms, you are configuring the behavior of the column, which provides various options for adjusting its width and justification. We will cover many of these **Layout** tools in a future chapter. During the course of our exploration, we will be familiarizing ourselves with many of these layout tools. Some of these tools do have complex features, but with use and practice, working with them will become a breeze.

Borders

Borders are a more straightforward tool than others, with the ability to control, depending on what the theme sets that include color, radius, and style.

Borders are a powerful way to show across a range of blocks, from buttons to images and others besides. Let's go through the steps of how you can adjust an image border:

1. As shown in *Figure 2.26*, add an Image block and pick any image you want. I am continuing to use the latest version of Twenty Twenty-Four in the examples using WordPress version 6.4.

Figure 2.26 – Design tools on an Image block

2. Go to the styles tab. Here, you can see options at the bottom for the border. As shown in *Figure 2.27*, select 8 px in the border settings to see what we are doing together clearly.

Figure 2.27 – Setting a border on an image

3. The observant among you will have noticed that you can do a few things, such as select **Default**, **Rounded**, and even **RADIUS** settings. **Default** and **Rounded** are something called *style variations* for the block, which are predefined styles that come with this block. **RADIUS** is a setting you can control through the styles tab.

    For this example, we are focusing on the **Border** settings, which include the size and radius. Let's also add a radius for a smoother experience. How about ramping things up and adding 80 px?

Figure 2.28 – Setting a radius on an image border

4. That looks like quite a neat effect for an image. One thing you can also do is impact just one side; remember the unlink option. This icon looks like a chain icon and when unlinked shows an open chain.

5. Click the **Unlink sides** to see your choices; add values of 80 px to the top and bottom to increase the impact.

Figure 2.29 – Adding some spacing with a border radius

6.   This now looks like an old film or photograph. It has created a nice little effect. Now, don't forget to save what you have done.

Button borders

While I just showed the impact of borders on an image, a ubiquitous border styling option is the one for buttons. For example, as shown in *Figure 2.30*, with a `100` px border, you can create a rounded button. We are also going to add a `1px` border and text color to the default style.

Figure 2.30 – Button block

In *Figure 2.31*, you can see a simple effect by using unlink and setting the border radius just on one side.

Figure 2.31 – Adjusting just one border on a button block

Explore more

What other fun things can you come up with by exploring these unlinking and linking combinations? Please give it a go yourself! Don't forget to save and preview.

Shadows

Shadows is a option from WordPress 6.2, so it is the least supported option for now in many themes. It is also only active, like many other features, when a theme supports it. It provides a box shadow feature, where you can set full and partial opacity, which can lead to some fun effects.

The **Shadow** option, as shown in *Figure 2.32*, can be seen in the theme Björk by Anders Norén, where the buttons have this style. You can explore this theme here: https://wordpress.org/themes/bjork/. This is shown using the Site Editing interface.

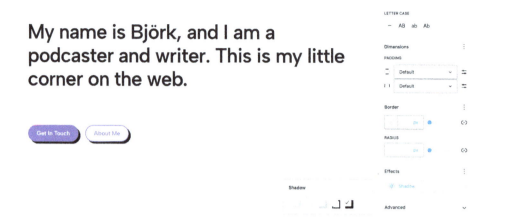

Figure 2.32 – Box shadow tool on a button

You can easily change one of the pre-configured options here or use the Style Book, which we will explore later in *Chapter 11*.

Here, you have a softer version, showing the difference that can be made using the box shadow presets in a theme.

Figure 2.33 – Another style of box shadow on a button

Shadows are a great way to elevate your design, and more themes are starting to support this feature.

That wraps up our journey through each design tool, but we're not done with this chapter yet. Now we are going to explore how to combine those tools and go even further.

Leveling up design tools

So far, we've looked at some simple design tools, often one at a time. In this section, we are going to look at how you might combine them and some tips along the way. That said, let's dive right in with an example to work on together.

Example 1 – a cover block

For this example, we will combine a **Cover** block with some typography tools, color, and other image treatments to get some exciting combinations. An effective **Cover** block can add impact on the to your content.

> **Did you know?**
>
> Did you know you can set the width of a block, depending on your theme, to go beyond the confines of your post? You can do this by clicking the align icon on the block toolbar. You will have different options here depending on your theme; in *Figure 2.34*, which uses Twenty Twenty-Four, we can see a wide range of options.

1. Select the **Cover** block from the block library and then add your image to this new block; for this example, we will set the alignment to be wide, as shown in *Figure 2.34*. Now, select a photo, and you will see the option to add some text. Put in some text so we can style it. We will do a few things in this example, including styling text and the background.

Figure 2.34 – Adjusting Cover block alignments

2. Once you add some text, you can use the steps we learned previously and open up the duotone tools. Remember these are in the block toolbar and the settings sidebar – the icon is shown in *Figure 2.35*, the circle with a half-shaded section. Set this to grayscale, and let's also do one more thing. Go to the gradient tools. Pick a gradient and apply it. By default, it will be at **50** overlay opacity; slide that down to **30** to give more subtle coloring on top of the grayscale. You can see the result of these steps in *Figure 2.35*.

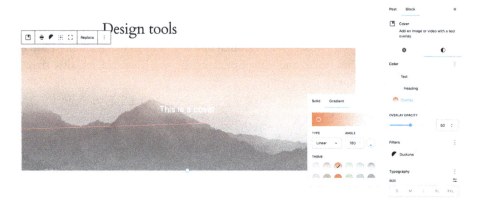

Figure 2.35 – Changing the overlay opacity

3.   By combining the duotone settings like this, we can reset an image and then add a gradient effect. This is a good base, but that text could do with some padding, so let's do that. Increase the size to XL using the typography size tools and set it to bold.

Figure 2.36 – Changing text size and weight

You can easily change the block type even within a block at any time by clicking the block's type icon in the block toolbar. Here you can switch in this example from the Paragraph Block to others such as Heading or List. This is known as 'transforming' the block and the options you get depend on what block you are using. The transforming icon is the second from the left in *Figure 2.37*.

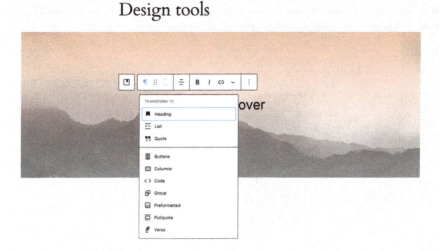

Figure 2.37 – Paragraph block transforming

We are getting somewhere, but that text is still quite hard to read at this size.

4.   One thing that the Cover block does well is it adjusts the color for you. Let's go back to the gradient tool and, as shown in *Figure 2.38*, increase the opacity to 80.

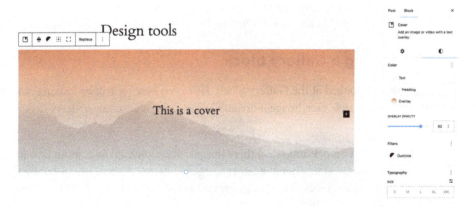

Figure 2.38 – Increasing opacity on the Cover block

This is a different look, but you can more clearly see the text, which, for this example, is helpful to improve readability. It can be hard to test contrast against gradients, so be sure to do that. By playing around with combinations like this, we can explore what we want – more strength or subtlety. The choice is yours.

5. The **Cover** block has a range of tools you can explore, such as focal point – give yourself some time to investigate setting different focal points to your image. Set the background to repeating (Repeated background) and see what combinations you can come up with. See *Figure 2.39*.

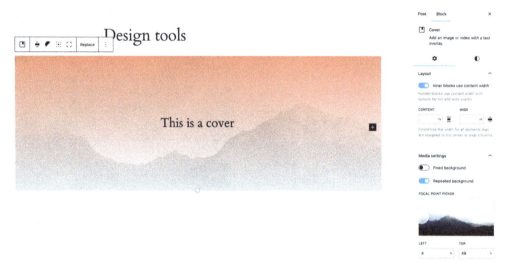

Figure 2.39 – Setting focal point on Cover block

6. Finally, don't forget to save and publish it to use. You can also copy and use it again within your content.

Now that we've done one example, let's go even further by styling a more complex block – **Gallery**.

Example 2 – styling a Gallery block

In previous examples, we looked at the **Gallery** block. However, here we will be looking at images. Did you know that you can style each image individually and create an exciting gallery? Let's see how that might work:

1. To start, add a **Gallery** block and select three images. Then, pick a two-column layout for the block using the side panel to place the larger image below. See *Figure 2.40*. A handy tip is to remember that a **Gallery** block is made up of Image blocks. So, using **List View**, you can select them all to be displayed in a list view and apply a 1 px border with an 6 px radius, just like this.

Figure 2.40 – Selecting multiple images in a Gallery block

2.   While this is great, it doesn't have much of an impact; let's bring some color to our images with some individual duotones. Return to each photo by clicking on them individually, and apply a duotone of your choice. We will also increase all borders to 2px when we do this.

Figure 2.41 – Applying duotone to all images

3. As you can see in *Figure 2.41*, this increases the impact of your gallery. Now, one thing you can do, because each image is individual, is to style the bottom picture with a more robust border. Let's do that now by increasing the border to 4 px.

Figure 2.42 – Setting a border on an image in a Gallery block

Using the contained blocks and their tools, as shown in *Figure 2.42*, you can create incredible combinations.

Copy and pasting styles

This relatively new feature – of being able to copy and paste a style you have created using design tools on any block – is quite handy. This goes beyond the simple design tools but is worth sharing early on in this journey as it opens up many possibilities.

In the following figure, you can see the **Copy styles** block option in the menu, again found through the more menu, or three-vertical-dots icon.

Figure 2.43 – Copy styles block option in menu

Copy and pasting styles like this is a great way to share your styles and use them on other blocks. It's just one feature of many being iterated on to make working with styling easier within WordPress.

Summary

We have journeyed through extensive information in this chapter and added to our knowledge; let's recap what we have covered:

- Discovered that what design tools are available depends on the theme you are using, to a certain extent.

- Learned how to set a custom value and individually reset those tools per type - for example, all colors.

- Learned about each design tool and how each design tool has a different interface, by showing an example per type.

- Discovered how to unlink tools, such as the sides of a button, to give just the bottom a border. This led into learning how to create interesting shapes using this knowledge.

- Learned how you can create incredible designs by combining design tools. We found out about each design tool and how to use them. As we explored, we discovered how much can be done through design tools that before needed knowledge of CSS.

We've taken our basic understanding from *Chapter 1* of the Block Editor and, in this chapter, added design tools and created some style combinations. In the next chapter, we are going to dive into block styles and explore both code and no-code options.

Questions

Answer the following questions to test your knowledge of this chapter:

1. What theme you are using impacts what design tools you have available.

    a. True

    b. False

2. Can you combine design tools on the same block?

    a. Yes

    b. No

3. Which of the following describes design tools?

    a. You can use design tools instead of CSS to style your blocks.

    b. Design tools are a plugin to add tools to your editor.

    c. Design tools are an experimental feature and none are available to use today.

Answers

1. What theme you are using impacts what design tools you have available.

    a. True

2. Can you combine design tools on the same block?

    a. Yes

3. Which of the following describes design tools?

    a. You can use design tools instead of CSS to style your blocks.

3

Block Styles

In the last chapter, we explored the power of design tools and walked through each of the tools themselves. We worked through examples together and created some blocks that combined styles together. Now, we are going to move on to looking at a feature called **block styles**.

In this chapter, we will cover the following topics:

- What is a block style?

- Removing a default block style

- Creating a theme using the **Create Block Theme** plugin

- Why would you create a custom block style

- Two approaches to create a block style

Together, we will learn to add and remove block styling with PHP and JavaScript. Unlike most chapters in the book, this one will require some coding. However, the coded sections will be explained in detail.

Technical requirements

To access the code used in this chapter, you can use this link: `https://github.com/PacktPublishing/WordPress-styling-with-blocks-patterns-templates-and-themes-/tree/main/Chapter-3`.

What is a block style?

A block style in WordPress refers to the appearance of a block within the editor. This could be any type of content, from a paragraph to an image or video.

A block style determines a wide range of visual attributes, from color and spacing to even font size. There are default block styles provided for each block type, but you can create your own or use plugins or themes that have their own presets. They are a great and easy method of creating styling for blocks.

> **Note**
>
> In this example, we are using the default theme Twenty Twenty-Four, and later in this chapter, we will use Twenty Twenty-Two. As stated previously, you can use any local setup you want to install this on.

If you do add a block style, that doesn't have to be the end of your customizations, either. If those settings are available in the theme, you can use the settings on the block on top of that to refine it. Each block style can be changed using a very simple interface. You can also preview it to see the style in action before you apply it.

Block styles are found under the **Block** settings tab in the side panel; you need to click on the **Styles** tab (the half-filled circle icon) to view the block style. In the following screenshot, you can see the default block style for the image block.

Figure 3.1 – Showing a preview of block style

This block also has a rounded corner style, which you can see and then apply by selecting the **Rounded** option under this section.

Block styles work by adding a CSS class to the block once you select them. At their core, block styles are simply a CSS class, but the ability to apply them using a visual interface that you can preview and simply click is where the magic happens. You can also register any number of styles for blocks – but remember, you do need to consider the impact on the user if there are too many styles layered on top of each other and what is useful.

You can see a CSS class added in the following screenshot. Under **Advanced** you can see **Additional CSS Class(es)** where **Plain** is active for the Styles and **is-style-plain** is applied there as a class. To see this, you need to have the quote block selected as in *Figure 3.2*.

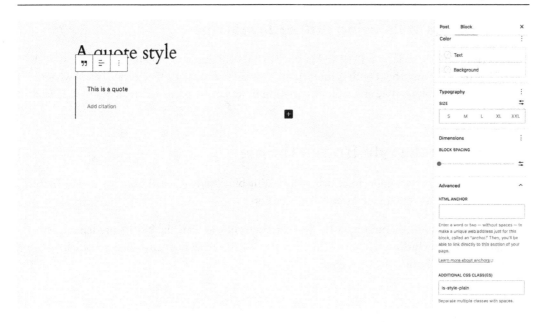

Figure 3.2 – A block style selected

Knowing when to create your own styles is key. Always check what your theme has available first, along with your site's settings. For example, WordPress does provide some basic settings, such as setting a border around the content. Consider which styles would be useful for your specific requirements – perhaps a fancy quote option?

Block variations

One point that is often confusing for those starting out with the editor is the difference between block styles and block variations:

- **Block styles**: These change the look of a block with CSS and can be applied through the side panel.
- **Block variations**: These change the block settings and create a variation of that original block with all its presets.

As you can see, block variations are powerful and a way to mix block styles. In this book, as our focus is going to be on as little code as possible, we won't be diving too far into all of these areas; there is a lot to cover. You can find more details about all of this within the official handbook here: `https://developer.wordpress.org/block-editor/reference-guides/block-api/block-variations/`.

Adding a block style using PHP or JavaScript

You can register a block style with PHP and JavaScript. We will share both methods. You most likely will see PHP, but knowing about both is important. Now we know what a block style is and what the difference between a block style and a block variation is, let's move on to adding a block style from a theme.

Adding a block style from a theme

For this walkthrough, we are going to be using an existing block style selected from the theme. In this task, we are going to use the theme **Twenty Twenty-Four**:

1. Let's start by adding a button block. You can then click to view the block's predefined styles called **Fill** and **Outline**. Here in *Figure 3.3*, you can see what happens when you click on the **Styles** tab and have a block selected.

Figure 3.3 – Adding a button with default style

2. Notice how it selects **Fill** first? This is handy to know the default style of the block. The other style is **Outline**.

3. Let's now change the block style. You can do that simply by clicking **Outline**, as shown in the following screenshot.

Figure 3.4 – Changing the block style

4. How good is that? Without needing to apply lots of styling, we have an outline style. This is all predefined in the theme and so is dependent on its creator.

5. If you want to go back, you can of course use undo in this case, or just simply click **Fill** at any point. You can also choose to create on top of this. For example, what about adding a color?

Figure 3.5 – Adding a color to a changed block style

As you can see, you can use block styles as a foundation on which to create even more. You think of block styles not just as something to set and be done with, but as something you can use to boost your work toward an entirely different look and feel.

Removing a default block style

For this example, we are going to begin our journey into code.

The first question might be, why would you want to remove a block style? Well, perhaps you have a theme you are working on that has a few block styles, and you want to add your own in place of them? Or perhaps you want to reduce the options available?

This is the start of our coding journey. If you don't want to add any code to your theme at all, you can skip to the next chapter.

> **Note**
> In these examples I have used the useful **Create Block Theme** plugin, taking the Twenty Twenty-Two theme this time as a base. With this amazing plugin, you can spin up your own theme. You can check it out here: `https://wordpress.org/plugins/create-block-theme/`.

Using the Create Block Theme plugin

In *Chapter 13*, we will explore many more of the options of this plugin, but for now, let's use some defaults to get up and running with it. Let's walk through the following steps to create our theme using Twenty Twenty-Two.

1. Make sure you have the default theme Twenty Twenty-Two activated. As noted, we are going to use this as our base.

2. Then, go to plugins and search for **Create Block Theme** and click **Install Now**, followed by clicking **Activate** once the plugin has been installed. You can see this in *Figure 3.6*.

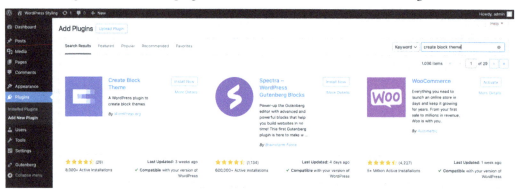

Figure 3.6 – The Create Block Theme plugin in the Add Plugins browser

3. Next, go to **Appearance** and then **Create Block Theme** to see the settings. In this case, we want to select **Clone** the theme to create our own version based on the theme in *Chapter 13*, we will go over these settings in more depth.

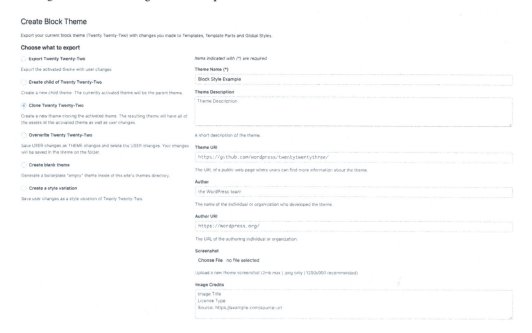

Figure 3.7 – Create Block Theme settings page

When filling in the options that appear after selecting **Clone**, ensure you add details to anything with an asterisk (*) beside it. So, in this case, we need to fill in the **Theme Name** field. As this example relates to block styling, we are going to call it `Block Styling Example`. Then click **Generate**, which is found right down on the bottom left.

That is all you must do to create your theme. Now, using a code editor of your choice, open the files that were created and downloaded on clicking **Generate**. In the example here, Visual Studio Code is going to be used.

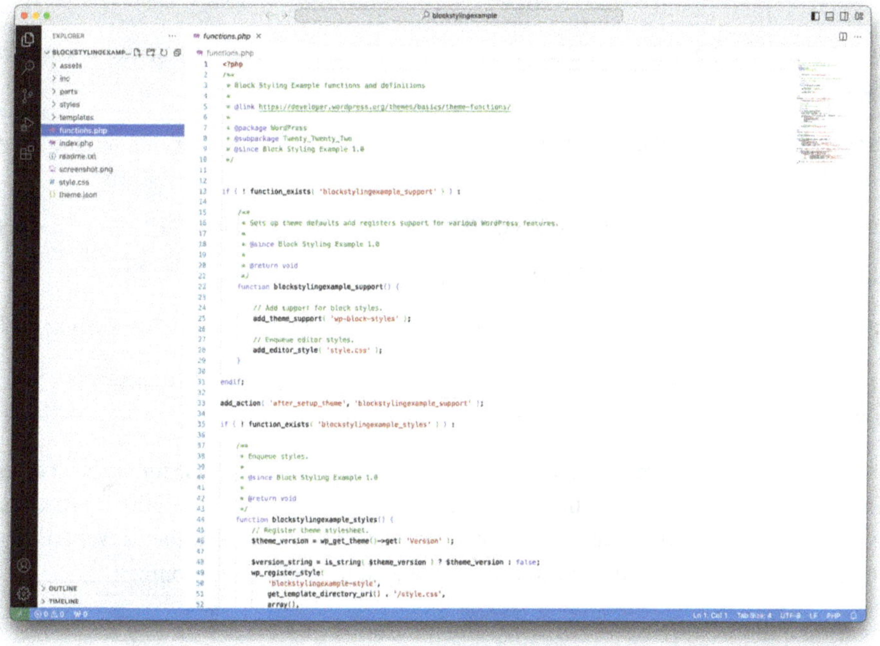

Figure 3.8 – The files for a new theme from the Create Block Theme plugin

Whether you choose to use PHP or JavaScript is up to your personal preferences when working with themes. We are going to cover examples of both so you can choose as you wish.

Using PHP

There are two methods we are going to use. Let's review those first:

- `wp_dequeue_style()` (https://developer.wordpress.org/reference/functions/wp_dequeue_style/) – This is used to remove a previously enqueued stylesheet.

- `wp_enqueue_scripts()` (https://developer.wordpress.org/reference/hooks/wp_enqueue_scripts/) – This is the hook to use when enqueuing scripts and styles to appear on the front of your site. To remove the script you are looking for the 'slug' of the block, which is the style handle to remove.

> **Slug**
>
> A slug is a string that identifies for example a block and can be the theme name, in our case with any spaces replaced by dashes.

Before we jump into our block style, let's cover some basics around registering and unregistering block styles:

- Our example to start will involve removing the block styles from the front end, not the selection in the Block/Site Editor.

- You can only unregister a block style via PHP if it has been added via PHP.

- Likewise, if you add a block style via JS, it needs to be removed via JS.

- You can't mix languages, for example, by adding block styles via JS and then removing via PHP.

Let's start by opening our code editor. In this example, we are going to use Visual Studio Code. We have two styles by default for the quote block in this theme: Default and Plain.

Not all themes have a `functions.php` file. The theme we are using as a base for our next example, Twenty Twenty-Two; comes with one. If you don't have this file, you have a few options. First, you can create your own; secondly, you can create a companion plugin to go with your theme. We aren't going to go through those steps here, but you can learn more with the following resources:

- Creating a theme `functions.php` file handbook guide: `https://developer.wordpress.org/themes/basics/theme-functions/`

- Creating a basic plugin WordPress: `https://developer.wordpress.org/plugins/plugin-basics/`

> **Note**
>
> Both of these links do presume some code knowledge, which is why it's worth starting with a theme as we are that comes with this for now.

1. Make sure you have activated the theme you just cloned and that it is ready to be used.

2. In order to add code to this theme, you have a few options. You can add the code within a code editor and upload it each time you save. You can also use the theme editor. Be sure to not use the built-in theme editor to edit any default theme files, but you can use it with theme files of your own creation that won't need auto-updating.

3. Add the following code to your `functions.php` file. The word "prefix" could be the name of your theme – for example `blockstylingexample`. If your theme doesn't have this file, create one at the theme root, which is where the `style.css` file is located.

```
function prefix_remove_core_block_styles() {
    wp_dequeue_style( 'wp-block-quote' );
}


add_action( 'wp_enqueue_scripts', 'prefix_remove_core_block_
styles' );
```

4. If you then view your theme, this will show in the editor the styles removed for that block. This is great, but all we have really done is stop them showing on the front as noted at the start of these steps.

This is great for block-by-block work. It is a bit more complicated to remove all styles – you can find the resource about that in the reference section.

If you want to do this via JavaScript you can use a similar path using the `unregister_block_style` function. It's worth noting this only works when `register_block_style` has been used. What this does is literally unregister a style. For example, if you had a style called `big-quote`, this would look as follows:

```
unregister_block_style( 'core/quote', 'big-quote' );
```

We aren't going to explore that here as our goal is to focus only a little on code and a full examination of this technique would go quite in-depth. However, you can follow the steps given in the following link on how to add to a `.js` file (the file type for JavaScript) and then call it within your PHP: `https://developer.wordpress.org/block-editor/reference-guides/block-api/block-styles/`. You will grow in confidence by exploring new methods like this, so it is strongly encouraged.

Why would you create a custom block style?

There are many reasons you might want to create your own custom style, including reusability and not wanting to set each style manually multiple times. You can of course copy some styles but having them in the block itself is useful.

There are a few parts to a custom block style you need to register:

- A unique name: `border-double`
- A label: `is-style-border-double`
- The CSS (style) you are going to be applying: `border-style: double`

Let's take this knowledge into some code exercises and create our own block style. It's worth noting that often, block styles are a bit more complex than the preceding example, where we applied simple styles using the existing options, or getting what we want by combining more than one style. For example, you would find adding a border to the entire image block is simple, so when thinking about what to create, think about what might not be possible using design tools so easily.

Approaches to creating a block style

There are two approaches to add styles. Let's review them now. As stated previously, you can use either PHP or JavaScript – which you use is entirely up to you. The examples in this book use a mixture of both for demonstration purposes. It's worth learning both and each has its merits typically based on what you want to achieve with a given theme style, but today a lot of themes use PHP, so let's start with that.

Along with these two languages, there are two approaches: one of declaring inline styling in the function for the block style, and another to have the function call a class inline. We are going to explore both.

Custom block style using PHP with inline CSS

Let's begin by looking at the function we are using:

register_block_style() PHP function:

`https://developer.wordpress.org/reference/functions/register_block_style/`

The format for this is as follows:

```
register_block_style(
    $block_name,
    $style_properties
);
```

Let's walk through the possible properties you can have:

- **name**: This is something called a "unique identifier" and generates the CSS class
- **label**: This is a label that is clear and able to be translated
- **inline_style**: The actual CSS to be printed
- **style_handle**: The handle of the stylesheet if enqueued for styling
- **is_default**: This sets whether this style should be the default or not

To start, we use `register_block_style()` to create a single style.

You have a few options for where the code and files go when using PHP. You can place it in a `functions.php` file or link to code in another file. For our example, we are going to add to a `functions.php` file.

1. Open up or create `functions.php`. If you have been following along from previous examples in this chapter, you can use the file we had previously. For this exercise, we are using our own theme that we cloned from Twenty Twenty-Two called `blockstylingexample` – this is our `themeslug`. If you want to call your theme anything else, you can swap those words out in your own code.

2. Add the following first to check whether the function exists:

```
if ( ! function_exists( 'blockstylingexample_block_styles' )
```

3. We will close this later on, but for now, go to the next line.

   Next, we are going to start with the function. The block style we are going to create here is a feature quote.

   We could bring in styling through CSS variables here, but let's keep it simple for now. The following is what we are going to do:

   - We are adding a border that uses a "groove" style set to 20px.

   - We use the `currentColor` value of the theme for the borders, which is whatever the theme specifies.

   - Then, we use `!important` this forces this style to be implemented. Not all themes will require this, but we do it for this block and its styling. You need to remember this trick but use it only when your styling doesn't apply. It's a way of forcing your styling to take precedence over the other styles in the theme.

   - Then we add some padding and increase the font size.

   You will notice we use `!important` here to force the styling. Some styling requires this and in testing it was within Chrome. Ensure you test all block styles when you create them to determine whether you need this.

4. Remember to close that out with the following:

```
endif;
add_action( 'init', 'blockstylingexample_block_styles' );
```

   This ensures you are ending what we started in *step 2*.

5. Save all of that and you should have the following in your file:

```
if ( ! function_exists( 'blockstylingexample_block_styles' ) ) :
   function blockstylingexample_block_styles() {
```

```
            register_block_style(
              'core/quote',
              array(
                'name' => 'feature-quote',
                'label' => __( 'Feature quote', 'blockstylingexample' ),
                'inline_style' => '
                  .is-style-feature-quote {
                    border: 20px groove currentColor!important;
                    font-size: 200%;
                    font-weight: bold;
                    padding: 10px;
                  }'
              )
            );
          }
        endif;
        add_action( 'init', 'blockstylingexample_block_styles' );
```

6.   Now, let's run that in our theme to see whether we can view the **Feature quote** style. See *Figure 3.9*. It's important to refresh the work within the editor as you create it if it's already open. You can use *Cmd + R* (Mac) or *Ctrl + F5* (on Windows) to reload the editor so the block style is loaded correctly.

Figure 3.9 – A new style added

7.   Let's now view this on the front end of the site to see it in action.

Figure 3.10 – Viewing the new style on the site

You might be wondering why the advice is to not edit a default theme using the theme file editor? This is because all the changes made by yourself can be overwritten and gone when the default theme receives an update. Not a great thing to happen to all your work! So, make sure not to edit default themes using the theme file editor. In our example, we have either been using this or a code editor such as Visual Studio Code. Let's continue by now using the theme file editor.

Access the theme file editor by going to `Tools > Theme File Editor` as shown in *Figure 3.9*. There is a strong warning here though – you are editing a live theme, so be aware that whenever you make any changes, you do avoid the issues you might encounter with uploading when working on styles or having to test things. For our examples, we are going to use this. We've covered a lot, but next let's see how to add a custom block style using PHP with its own stylesheet file. This is a more recommended method as it is the simplest option.

Custom block style using PHP with a stylesheet

Previously, we used an inline style, which is great, but depending on your preference you can achieve the same thing by adding a stylesheet and it helps if you have multiple inline styles which might not scale. This is why many prefer to use a stylesheet over inline declarations in the function. Let's look at how we can use stylesheets now:

1. First, we return to our file `functions.php` file and the function defined previously. This time, let's edit in the theme file editor so you can see it in action. Let's remove the `inline_style` property so we end up with the following:

Figure 3.11 – The block style removed on the quote block

2. Next, you would take the custom CSS and add to your style. For now, we have no custom CSS attached to the style; this is just the default quote style. We will now add that style back by creating an empty file to put it in. As you will probably have more than one style, it's useful to create your stylesheet under a folder called `assets` A file called `block-styles.css`. You can of course choose any solution here. Some people like to name it the same as the core file and have individual CSS; it's up to you. Another option that might be good is to add a folder called `custom` to add the `assets` folder in. You could also call this `styles` – it's up to you, and looking at how other themes do this is a great way to learn.

Let's look at what this looks like when you add the style:

Figure 3.12 – Updating the CSS for the class of the block style

3.   Our final step before viewing our work is to link up the stylesheet to make sure it gets loaded. Go back to functions.php and add the following:

```
if ( ! function_exists( 'blockstylingexample_enqueue_block_
styles' ) ) :
  function blockstylingexample_enqueue_block_styles() {
    wp_enqueue_block_style( 'core/quote', array(
      'handle' => 'blockstylingexample-is-feature-quote',
      'src'    => get_parent_theme_file_uri( 'assets/custom/
        block-styles.css' ),
      'ver'    => wp_get_theme( get_template() )->get( 'Version'
),
      path'    => get_parent_theme_file_path( 'assets/custom/
        block-styles.css' ),

    ) );
  }
add_action( 'init', 'blockstylingexample_enqueue_block_styles'
);
endif;
```

Let's review what we are doing above. We are adding the new stylesheet and enqueuing it, then we are asking it to be loaded when the theme loads.

4. Now, save your work. The method you use to do this depends on whether you're using a code editor, the theme file editor, or you need to upload your files to your server if using web hosting. Then you can view what you have done on your site by refreshing and ensuring you have the block style selected.

> **Note**
>
> Want to know more about using multiple styles for the same block? This has actually been possible since WordPress 5.9. Find out more here: `https://make.wordpress.org/core/2021/12/15/using-multiple-stylesheets-per-block/`

JavaScript approaches

We've now covered the various ways to create block styles in PHP. Let's dive into how you would approach this in JavaScript. It's about the same.

To create a custom block style in JavaScript you need to create a file, then enqueue it, much as we did with PHP, except this time with the following dependencies: wp-blocks, wp-demo-ready, and wp-edit-post. You will be using enqueue_block_editor_assets, about which you can learn more here: `https://developer.wordpress.org/reference/hooks/enqueue_block_editor_assets/`

In this example, we are using the same theme and folders as before. We are going to be adding to the js folder under assets. If you are using the same theme, remember to comment out the code used to add the block style previously, or simply remove it.

To comment out something in PHP you can use two methods:

- `// comments out a single line`
- `/** comments out the content of several lines and allows you to wrap around a larger block of code which you might not want to display **/`

We need to load the styles just as we did when using PHP. This is done in functions.php again with the following code:

```
function blockstylingexample_enqueue_block_editor_assets() {
  wp_enqueue_script(
    'blockstylingexample-block-js',
    get_stylesheet_directory_uri() . '/assets/js/block-styles.js',
    array( 'wp-blocks', 'wp-dom-ready', 'wp-edit-post' ),
    filemtime( plugin_dir_path( __FILE__ ) . '/assets/js/block-styles.
      js' )
```

```
    );
}
add_action( 'enqueue_block_editor_assets', 'blockstylingexample_
enqueue_block_editor_assets' );
```

Our goal is to have a file specifically for block styles and a function being called purely for that purpose. It's often easier to split it out like this to know what is loading where. You can take any number of approaches here – explore more at the following link: https://developer.wordpress.org/block-editor/reference-guides/block-api/block-styles/

Let's now see what this looks like within the theme file editor.

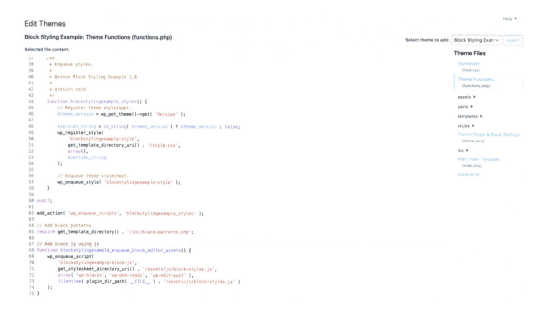

Figure 3.13 – Function to load JavaScript

Now, in your js file you need to add a registration to match that code you have the following:

```
wp.blocks.registerBlockStyle( 'core/quote', {
    name: 'feature-quote',
    label: 'Feature Quote'
} );
```

It looks like this:

Figure 3.14 – JavaScript block style

We are simply going to register here our style, not add any styling. You might now be asking yourself; how do we do that? Well, we have a style already, so let's use that stylesheet and enqueue it in our `functions.php` file so it looks like the following:

Figure 3.15 – Adding in the CSS and function to call the JavaScript block style

Let's now go and open the editor once we've saved our files and see whether this works.

Figure 3.16 – JavaScript block style in editor

There we go – it's just as before, but this time we did it all using JavaScript. How cool is that?

> **Tip**
> Don't forget; if you want to de-register a JavaScript block style you need to do through JavaScript.

Summary

This chapter has taken us on an adventure to discover the capabilities of block styles. We have seen how to add already existing styles, how to create styles using code, and some different methods to this. Not only did we walk through some step-by-step examples, but we also dived right in by adding some code to the theme itself.

Let's recap the great expanse of things we have tackled together:

- We used a block style that is already present in a default theme.
- We customized that block style by adding a color to the style.
- We explored some code together for the first time and looked at the various approaches of adding a block style, learning how to do this using PHP and JavaScript.
- We created code and applied it to remove a single block style.
- We learned how to add a block style using PHP and two different approaches for styling.

Now that you have all of this under your belt, you can create your own block styles and customize existing themes as required.

In the next chapter, we will move on from individual blocks and look at how we can combine them to create patterns. Whilst blocks are powerful, their true power multiplies when we start adding them into patterns.

Questions

Answer the following questions to test your knowledge of this chapter:

1. Which of the following statements explains the difference between a block style and block variation?

    a. A block style changes the look of a block with CSS and can be applied through the side panel. A block variation changes the block settings or creates a variation of that original block with all its presets.

    b. A block style and block variation are the same thing. The only difference is that block styles are loaded in a plugin and block variations are loaded in the theme.

2. Can you use both PHP and JavaScript to load a block style?

    a. Yes

    b. No

3. If you load a block style using PHP, you have to remove it using PHP. True or false?

    a. False

    b. True

4. Can you apply styles on top of a block style?

    a. Yes

    b. No

Answers

1. Which of the following statements explains the difference between a block style and block variation?

    a. A block style changes the look of a block with CSS and can be applied through the side panel. A block variation changes the block settings or creates a variation of that original block with all its presets.

2. Can you use both PHP and JavaScript to load a block style?

    a. Yes

3. If you load a block style using PHP, you have to remove it using PHP. True or false?

    b. True

4. Can you apply styles on top of a block style?

    a. Yes

Further reading

If you want to discover more about removing default block styles, there is a more in-depth guide here: https://fullsiteediting.com/lessons/how-to-remove-default-block-styles

4

Blocks and Styles Wrap-Up

So far, we have looked at the power of styling blocks, and this chapter is going to wrap that up. Together, we have discovered a great deal about using design tools and the concept of block styles, from learning what blocks are and discovering the design tools on offer to then applying this knowledge via some working examples. We then explored block styles and how you can add, remove, and work with them with both JavaScript and PHP.

Taking all that knowledge with us, we are now going to close our exploration of singular blocks with a chapter that looks at what they are today and where they are going in the future by combining everything we have learned. We will also examine the constantly changing state of design tools. Blocks are the foundation of WordPress content creation and styling them opens up a world of possibilities.

In this chapter, we will look into the following:

- Unleashing creativity
- The evolution of design tools
- Tips and tricks

From our examination of blocks in this chapter, we will move in the next chapter to patterns, which combine blocks together.

Unleashing creativity – combining design tools

In the previous chapters, we already looked at how you can combine design tools to create some powerful combinations. We are now going to build on that knowledge by considering some advanced combinations of design tools in an example together.

Some common things typically required when styling might not be present in your theme, but don't worry – you can create versions of various styling effects fairly easily without touching any code. Combining effects is something truly powerful. In the following example, let's look at how we can create some borders to mimic shadows and stack this with other styles.

Effects on groups to create shadows

If your theme doesn't have a shadow option, there's no need to worry – you can create a border on a single side and create the impression of a shadow. In the following example, we are going to create a bottom border using two methods. Let's get started:

1. We are going to create a column block first to contain everything. Let's add one. The first step with a column block is picking the variation you want – we want a three-column block with an equal split, so click that option to add it.

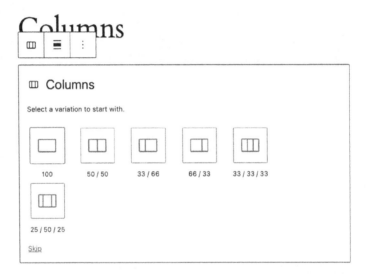

Figure 4.1 – Adding a column block

2. In the column, add a header, paragraph, and button. Copy this into each column to build them up with some content. Don't forget that you can always use the **List View** option to get an overview of the structure of your work.

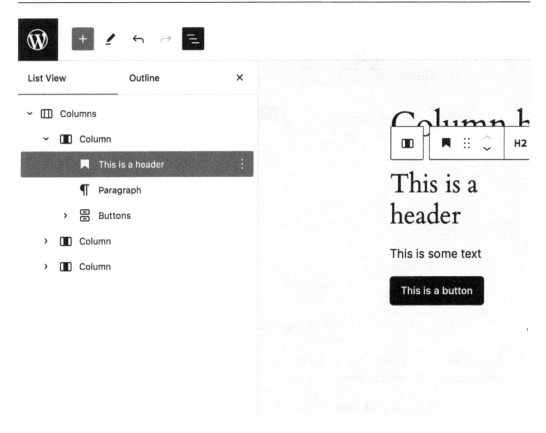

Figure 4.2 – Using the list view to see what is going on

3. Next, we are going to look at adding a border to a column. If you add a border around just one column section, visually, you will run into the next column. You can avoid this by adding padding.

4. Let's now do that by adding some padding to the column using the design tool. Let's also add a border around the content to end up with what we see in the following screenshot.

Figure 4.3 – A full border around the group

5.   Remember, you can unlink the border so you can just add to the bottom border and like this add a background color and some padding. To "unlink" just click the chain icon to the side.

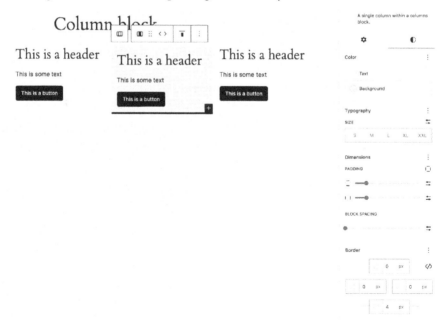

Figure 4.4 – A bottom border and styling

6. Now that we've created quite an impact with one column, let's work on the next one. We can choose different styling here, adding a different border to the bottom of the column compared to the other sides, along with some padding and a striking background color.

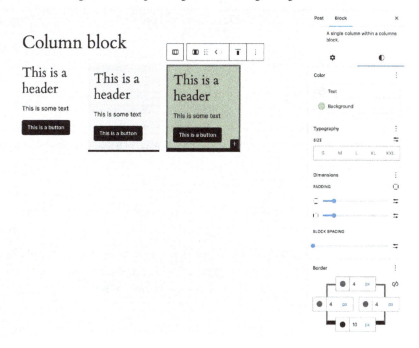

Figure 4.5 – Styling the border radius

7. Let's now color the background to add a difference to this section. Click the background and then you can use the **Styles** tab to change the color.

Once you have done that, let's try one last thing. Set the columns block to **Wide width** using the toolbar and preview. You can see this setting in *Figure 4.6*.

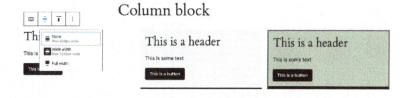

Figure 4.6 – Setting alignment to Wide width

This example showed how you can style borders for high impact. One thing to be careful of with blocks like this is that if you have different contents, they will vary in height, so the effect won't appear equal.

We've seen how you can experiment with unlinking borders and other elements to develop style variations. Now we are going to look at how design tools are evolving and gaining new features.

Design tools are evolving

Whilst we have listed a few design tools in this book so far, that's not where the journey stops. Design tools are part of the solution to one of the challenges that WordPress tries to tackle – *that of creating a design system based on components that is at the heart of a system that everyone can create with*. As more design tools are added, they combine to create a powerful toolkit that can be applied to blocks.

Sidebar controls and component system

Having solid unified patterns for things such as border controls (e.g., width and spacing) means you can then trust across all areas.

In the next screenshot, you can see the padding options set on a block. To get to these options, click on the padding options button, which is a rectangle with a horizontal line above it. By default, the granular padding options are grouped by horizontal and vertical settings – this can be changed, as shown in the following screenshot.

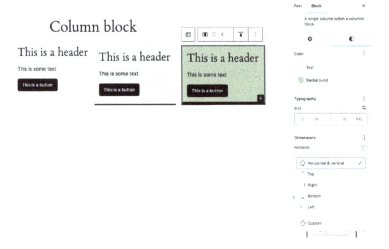

Figure 4.7 – An example of unified design tools

You can see in the preceding screenshot, the tool options can be grouped as one, or split out to adjust each one independently of the others. Using unlinked styling like this opens a world of possibilities.

Growing the blocks and tools

At the time of writing this, there are a few proposed tools and blocks. These even include a marquee – if you want to travel right back to the days of early web design! Of course, not every block or design tool should be accepted – the issue here is adopting only those that are useful.

Improvements to existing tools

It's not just new blocks or tools being added either – existing components like the **color picker** and typography tools are being developed iteratively. This means you can rely on them more and create powerful combinations.

There is already a way to specify the language of a piece of text, which many don't know about as an example of things you can do now that you couldn't before. This is useful if you want to only change one section and the displays depending on the block, in the following example you can see for the Paragraph block. Let's walk through how to use this together:

1. Highlight any text in the editor, and then from the drop-down arrow, select **Language**.

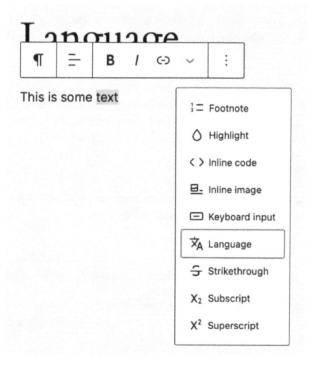

Figure 4.8 – Setting the language on a paragraph block

2. From here, you can then select the option to change **Language** and the text direction it uses, such as left to right or right to left.

Figure 4.9 –The language options

Powerful tools such as text manipulation and others result in us having to do less with custom CSS and more with the block itself, which empowers more users to create the layout they want.

Adding options

There have been more design tools added that are increasing what can be done with site editing. For example, you can place a "sticky" or fixed header or footer. With the recent additions, this can now be applied to any element. By doing this, you can unlock incredible layouts.

Create a sticky cover block

Sticky position was something requested by many for a long time, as it is often hard to do. It required either a theme option, plugin, or custom scripting knowledge. Now, you can unlock this power yourself with a few simple steps and apply it to a block.

For this example, we are going to use the default theme Twenty Twenty-Three. Exploring different default themes helps us gain familiarity with the workings of the system, so let's do just that:

1. First, we are going to add a cover block, set it to full-width alignment, and then add an image. Alignments can be specified for blocks using the block toolbar. Select the block, go to the toolbar, and then set the alignment to full width.

Figure 4.10 – A full-width cover image block

2. Now we can add some styles. Let's add a duotone and bring in some opacity with an orange overlay. This gives the sea-and-sunset image a bigger impact. Both duotone and overlay options can also be found in the Styles tab in the sidebar.

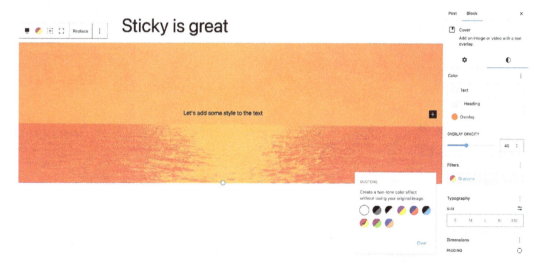

Figure 4.11 – Setting the color opacity and a duotone for the cover

3. We are now going to apply the sticky position. To do this, add a border around the group and then set the position to **Sticky** within the sidebar in the settings tab.

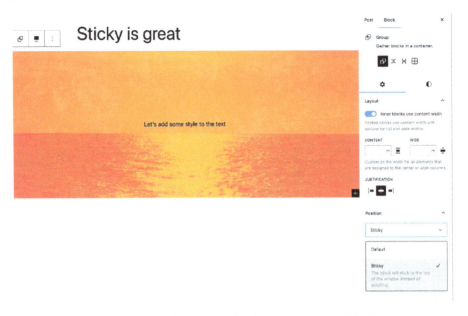

Figure 4.12 – Adding a group block around the cover block

4. Previewing is great to do at this point to see the impact. Let's add a gallery to see the sticky position in action.

Figure 4.13 – What you should see so far on the frontend

Try scrolling and you will see the gallery block move underneath the sticky cover. For greater visual impact, we have set the gallery to monotone using the duotone effect. It's powerful for front-page design to create a high-impact header and a monotone gallery like this.

5. Now we can style the text a little in the cover block to add some more power to the text and make it more striking. Set the color, font size, and weight to create the style as shown in *Figure 4.14*.

Figure 4.14 – Adding some text with a style

6. Once you save your work, preview it.

Figure 4.15 – Previewing everything done in browser

As you can see, the sticky positioning keeps the cover block in place with the gallery moving underneath it.

Whilst new things are great, we've also seen that additions and improvements to existing blocks and tools can come together to create a powerful suite of design features to empower users. So much is now possible that, before, required complex styles and scripts to achieve.

Let's move on and explore some tips and tricks for working with blocks and styling.

Tips and tricks

Applying styles and tools is fun, but what if you need to take a step back and review the structure of your design, for troubleshooting purposes or just clarity? Let's look at some tips and tricks as we close this chapter on block styling.

Copying to unpick

If you find a stacked style or combination has an issue, but you're unsure which piece to remove, rather than deleting everything, you can copy the block and unpick it style by style to work out what the issue is. This way, you can reduce the active styles to the specific problematic ones and then fix them.

> **Note**
>
> Remember that when things get complex, you can copy blocks using **List View** or use the contextual menu on the block toolbar to easily find the block.

In the following example, we are selecting the block and copying it using **List View**. This allows you to then unpick each style and work out where the problem lies – all without impacting the original block.

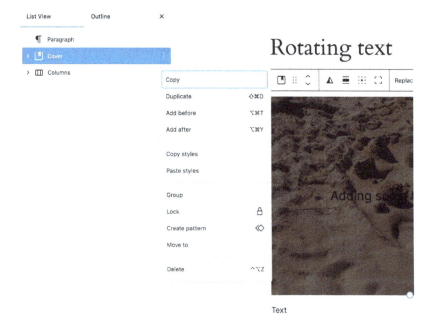

Figure 4.16 – Finding a block in List View and selecting Copy

You can work out styling issues by going over the styling; stepping back to the original block. One approach is to take a copy or use duplicate, then step back through the changes by turning them off one by one. The **Copy** function only creates copies and doesn't duplicate. **Duplicate** is a great option to insert right below a block.

Using text and background colors to override the theme

If you want to style a separator or border but you don't want to add custom CSS, or you haven't got that custom value in your theme, you can do this using the text value in colors for borders and background for separators.

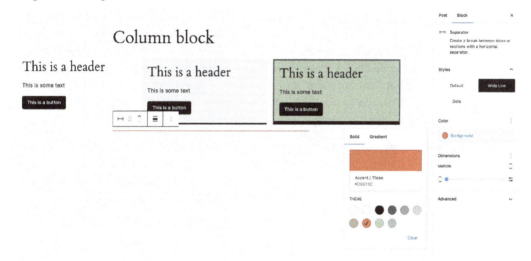

Figure 4.17 – Setting a background color to change separators

Adding colors like this can enable separates to either stand out or become unified with your theme styling. As you can see, exploring all the settings available to you from colors through to other tools is a great way to get to know your theme and how each block can appear.

Always preview!

Perhaps one of the foundational things to remember is: always preview your changes. What the editor shows you is close to the actual browser view, sometimes it might vary, so it's always worth checking. This is particularly true of different devices.

The following screenshot shows the use of the drop-down menu options for previews on desktop, tablet, mobile, and in a new tab. This menu appears after clicking on the laptop icon next to the **Publish** button.

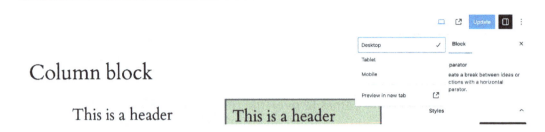

Figure 4.18 –Different device options to preview your work

block.json and block styles

We haven't introduced the concept of `block.json` yet, and whilst we aren't going to directly create blocks in this book, we can add block styles there. This is a slightly more advanced topic for those not looking to code, and you can find more details about this file and block styles here: `https://developer.wordpress.org/block-editor/reference-guides/block-api/block-metadata/#block-styles`.

Using `block.json` is really useful if you create a new block and want to add a block style. In our examples, we looked at adding a block style for an existing core block. If you want to create a new block, you can easily add variations within the `block.json` file and use custom CSS. In simple terms, the `block.json` file is the *recipe* that the block follows to create itself.

You would then need to reflect the block style class within the CSS to ensure that had styles. Whilst this is an additional topic, it might be one you want to explore if you investigate making blocks or ever have an issue finding where a style is.

Summary

We've covered a lot in the past few chapters about blocks, from looking at blocks themselves to styles and the design tools that can be combined to create incredible combinations.

Let's recap what we now can do after our exploration together:

- We have created a complex pattern using border styling and colors to apply effects to groups.
- We learned about additional design tools and the new features being developed.
- Together, we created a sticky cover block to showcase a new feature that was previously only capable with complex styling.

In this chapter, we discovered new tips and tricks related to styling blocks. Now we are ready to move on to patterns and explore how, when you start combining blocks, you truly unlock the power of creativity.

Questions

Answer the following questions to test your knowledge of this chapter:

1. Can you add block styles to a `block.json` file?

    a. Yes

    b. No

2. You always have to set borders on all sides of a group; you can never just set one. True or false?

    a. False

    b. True

3. How do you set a sticky position?

    a. Using CSS is the only way.

    b. You can use a sticky position setting within the advanced section.

Answers

1. Can you add block styles to a `block.json` file?

    a. Yes

2. You always have to set borders on all sides of a group; you can never just set one. True or false?

    a. False

3. How do you set a sticky position?

    b. You can use a sticky position setting within the advanced section.

Part 2: Block Patterns

Block patterns are the power of blocks combined, literally. They often are what people think of when visualizing their site. In this part, you will learn how to create them and discover them for yourselves.

This section has the following chapters:

- *Chapter 5, Understanding Block Patterns*
- *Chapter 6, Discovering and Creating Block Patterns*
- *Chapter 7, Discovering the WordPress Pattern Directory*
- *Chapter 8, Wrapping Up Patterns*

5

Understanding Block Patterns

In the previous chapters, we looked at blocks and the design tools you can use on them. The focus was on styling a single block Now, we are going to move beyond just one block and will look at how blocks can be even more powerful when they come together to form patterns, creating even more options.

In this chapter, we will unlock together the following:

- What is a block pattern?
- The power of block patterns

So, let's jump into what a block pattern is and start our journey into what happens when blocks come together.

What is a block pattern?

To put it simply, a block pattern is a collection of blocks. These blocks can have their own styles joined together and be shared, synced, and reused across themes.

Here, you can see an example of a pattern, which shows how useful they can be in providing the complete design piece you are looking for in your theme:

Figure 5.1 – Pattern from the Twenty Twenty-Two default theme

 A benefit of patterns is that they are just blocks with self-contained styled. Patterns are by their nature portable, because of this approach to styling. They can be copied and pasted easily. This means you can even copy one from the pattern directory, which we will discover a little later and use it right in your own content.

The power of block patterns

There are several benefits of block patterns. *The first is simply that it's easier to think in larger sections than a block.* When you consider a visual site, you think of visual sections, not the small block sections – for example, a feature content bucket pattern across a page, or anything else you want. Because these are larger visual sections, they build up faster to create the site.

It is important to distinguish between patterns and templates, though.

If you were to think of the hierarchy, it would be as follows:

- **Blocks**: The smallest content piece – for example, a paragraph or a quote
- **Patterns**: Collections of blocks – for example, a featured content area or a speaker list
- **Templates**: A full layout for an entire area – for example, a post or a page

Figure 5.2 – Another pattern from the default Twenty Twenty-Two theme

Patterns are portable; you can copy and paste them and put them in a theme to reuse. This means many themes come with their own patterns, which is really exciting.

Patterns are also syncable as of WordPress 6.3. This means you can keep your custom styling unified across instances of them. We will discover what this means a little later. Syncing brings even more power to patterns, enabling you to create portable, repeatable, customized patterns.

Discovering patterns in the editor

Let's explore how you find patterns within the editor. To do this, first, open a post within the editor or a page – you can add patterns either in the Block Editor or Site Editor. Depending on where you open the editor, the patterns are available for those experiences.

> **Note**
>
> Certain themes and plugins have patterns, so depending on the theme you have available, it might change your patterns showing in the view.

Let's look at how you can discover patterns by walking through the process together:

1.   Under the + button in the toolbar, click **Patterns**. Typically, this is how you would add a block from the top, but let's add a pattern. This method is good as you get to see the patterns easier.

     Let's look at the **Patterns** interface together in the next figure:

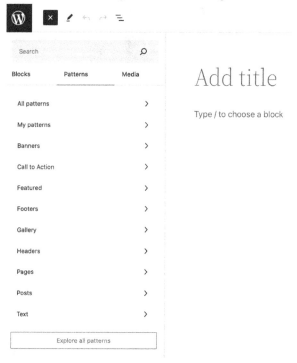

Figure 5.3 – The Patterns interface

2. From here, we are going to click on a category. Typically, when a pattern is added, it will have a category assigned. We will explore that together later. For example, here, in *Figure 5.4*, you can see this theme has **Featured** patterns:

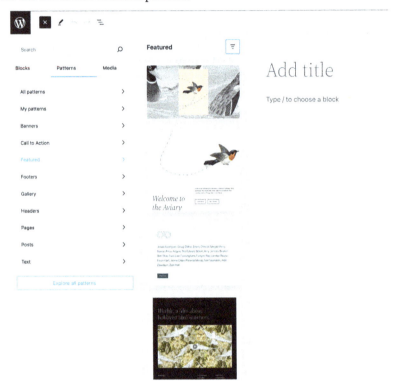

Figure 5.4 – The Featured patterns of Twenty Twenty-Two

You will notice there is an **Explore all patterns** button. This enables a different, richer browsing interface for patterns. Let's click that.

3. The interface that opens is a modal that shows all the patterns, like the thin sidebar but easier to see patterns in their full experience.

Figure 5.5 – The pattern browsing modal

From here, select a pattern and add it by clicking it.

4.   The pattern auto-adds to the content, and you can click in to edit right away, getting all the benefits of the preset styling and blocks:

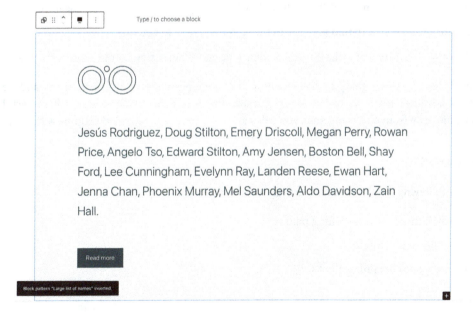

Figure 5.6 – A pattern added

This is how easily you can bring in custom styling at a higher, more complete level than doing it block by block, enabling you to create the layout you want faster and achieve that perfect site vision. Once you've added your pattern, don't forget to preview it, and then you're all set to use the new pattern.

As you can imagine, creating even such a simple pattern manually would have taken you longer than a simple click to add it. This is the true power of patterns! Not only is it fast to add, but it comes styled perfectly for the theme you are using as you pick a theme – specific one.

> **Note**
> It's worth noting that the design tools are still available, so should you not quite like a pattern, it's not permanent. You can, of course, add and iterate from there – already gaining the boost of styling as a foundation to work from.

Summary

In this chapter, we learned about a new concept: patterns. Where blocks are singular, patterns group them together and add styling, which offers a world of possibilities and makes it faster and easier to create the site you want.

Let's recap what we have learned after exploring this concept together:

- We understand what patterns are.
- We know that patterns are different from blocks and templates and that each has its purpose.
- We are aware of how to find patterns in the editor and how to add one.
- We know that themes often have patterns, which means we can customize our content even more.

In the next chapter, we are going to discover how to create block patterns and share them, and we will explore advanced concepts such as syncing and adding to a theme. Patterns are really powerful and, as we move up from blocks together, you will start to see your designs and ideas grow with them.

Questions

Answer the following questions to test your understanding of this chapter:

1. Which of these definitions fits a pattern?

    a. A collection of blocks

    b. A template containing blocks

2. By scale, which is the correct order of the following?

    a. Patterns, blocks, templates, and template parts

    b. Blocks, patterns, template parts, and templates

    c. Block, templates, patterns, and template parts

3. Is the following statement true or false? Some default themes have patterns.

    a. False

    b. True

Answers

1. Which of these definitions fits a pattern?

    a. A collection of blocks

2. By scale, which is the correct order of the following?

    b. Blocks, patterns, template parts, and templates

3. Is the following statement true or false? Some default themes have patterns.

    b. True

6

Discovering and Creating Block Patterns

In the previous chapter, we learned what block patterns are and how they build up from blocks to more meaningful sections, making it easier to add to your content. In this chapter, we are going to learn together how to create block patterns.

This chapter will investigate the following:

- Creating your own patterns
- Sharing your patterns
- Creating your own patterns and sharing them in a theme
- Reusable blocks and synced patterns
- Detaching a pattern
- Using the reusable blocks section for patterns

We will learn how to create block patterns step by step. After that, we are going to move on to how to share them both within an existing site and others. Then we will wrap up by looking at reusable and synced patterns together. The result of all of this will be building on our understanding of patterns to apply them.

Creating your own patterns

Creating patterns is easy, and you can do this within the interface. Let's dive in by creating a pattern by just using the interface. You can do this now. Previously, you had to create a pattern and then save it in a theme. Now you can manage everything within the editor itself – cool! For this example, we will use Twenty Twenty-Four as a theme as we have done in other walk-throughs.

1. Let's create a simple pattern by selecting a group block. We will use a new post or page to do this to start afresh. Most patterns start with a container of some form. The group block, cover, or columns are great foundations. Of course, you can try different options as well. As you can see in this screenshot, once you select that block, you have the option to add other blocks inside.

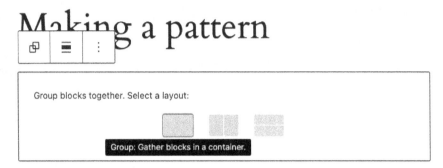

Figure 6.1 – A group block to create a pattern

2. Let's take the preceding block and add some things inside. We're going to add a header – selecting the H2 version, a paragraph, and a button. For now, this isn't styled – we are going to add styling later.

Figure 6.2 – A group block ready to make a pattern

As you can see, that is simple. Let's now add some basic styling. In the example we are going to use, let's do the following:

- Set the background to dark.

- Set padding around the entire group block.

- Change the color of the button.

- Set the width to "wide".

- Change the color of the header and paragraph text.

You can see those changes done in the following screenshot.

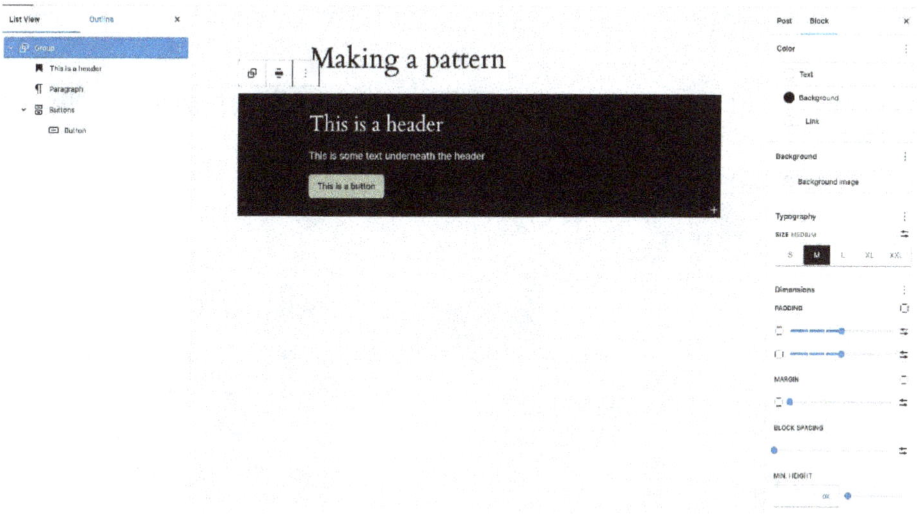

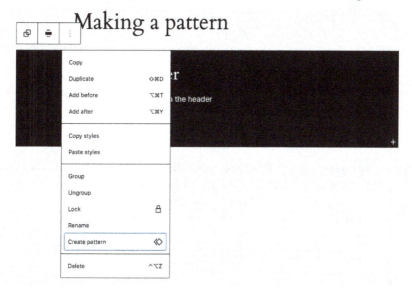

Figure 6.3 – Styling a the pattern

There we go!

3. We now want to select **Create pattern** from the more menu – the menu with the three vertical dots, within the block's toolbar – to do exactly that. You can see that in the following screenshot. What this does is take us through a series of screens. We will do a walkthrough of this together.

Figure 6.4 – The group block menu opens to create a pattern

As you can see, there are many options at this point, including copying – this would take the entire group and copy it to share just like a pattern. For now, though, let's focus on creating that pattern.

4. Once you select **Create pattern**, you get a modal that has a few fields to guide you through the process, as shown in the following screenshot.

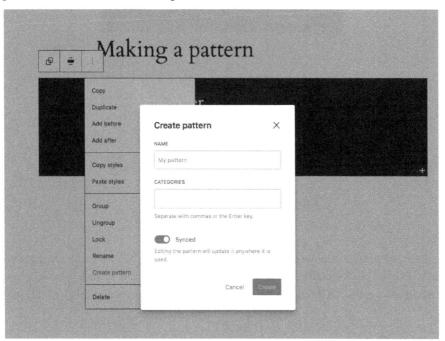

Figure 6.5 – The Create pattern interface

5. From here, you fill in **NAME**, **CATEGORIES**, and, by default, **Synced** is on. We will discover more about syncing later. When considering whether to sync or not, it's a good idea to think about whether you are going to reuse it exactly as is or make changes to the styling. It will default to **Synced**.

Now, let's add a few categories. A word of caution here: try and avoid creating too many categories at this stage. You can easily have too many and end up not knowing which refers to what. Keeping these simple and aligned with those of the WordPress pattern directory helps you. You can see some added along with a clear name in the next screenshot.

> **Note**
>
> The following screenshot has "banner" and "cta" on purpose for categories. This is to illustrate a point around case. The categories are case sensitive so if you can easily end up with multiple categories of similar names. Checking what your theme already uses is important to avoid this. Whilst you can edit them later, it's easier to start using the same ones for the same type. In this case we have a 'Banner' already so change it to that and "CTA".

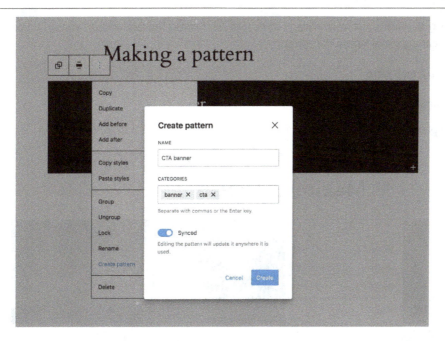

Figure 6.6 – Adding categories to a new pattern

Once you have all of those added, just click **Create** and your pattern will be created for you.

6. The pattern looks a little different, with a new icon, as you can see in the toolbar.

Figure 6.7 – The changes in menu options when a pattern is created

This now shows that it's a pattern. By clicking the "more" menu in the toolbar (shown by three dots), you have a new range of options added for that pattern, including **Manage patterns** and **Detach**.

Let's save this for now as we are going to discover how to share patterns and then look at ways to manage and detach them later.

Sharing your patterns

An easy way to share is just by copying your pattern. This works the same as how you would copy and paste content normally within the editor.

Sharing by copying

In this example, we are going to share a pattern by copying.

Select the pattern, go to the toolbar, and simply select **Copy**, as shown in this screenshot:

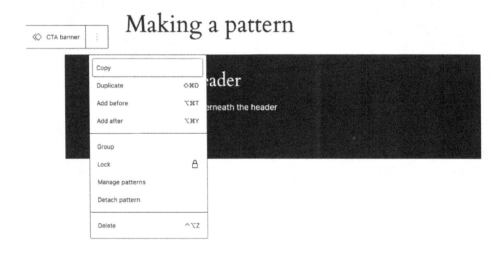

Figure 6.8 – A pattern selected to copy

From here, it will simply grab everything about that pattern. This stores it on the clipboard on your computer, ready to be pasted into another WordPress site or even a code editor – the output would be different within a code editor. It's that easy! Pretty cool, right?

Viewing in the editor

There are other ways you can share patterns, and many of those start by viewing them within the editor. You can do that in a couple of different places:

- In the editor itself
- Within the Site Editor pattern browser

Let's look at both options.

As we've seen in a previous chapter, just like patterns you bring in from any other place, you can find your own patterns right there in the browser. An example of this is in the side panel or the modal within the Site Editor. Each of your patterns (the patterns you created) gets a section called **My patterns**, along with any it belongs to.

Here, you can see it in the modal in the following screenshot. To open this modal, just click **My patterns** when within the **Patterns** browser modal.

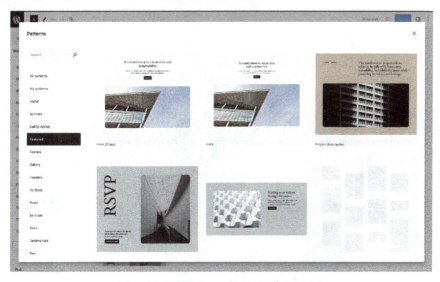

Figure 6.9 – Viewing patterns in the modal

This, again, has the same categories and everything, just like any other pattern. You can see all the details.

A newer interface outside the editor though, where you can find all patterns, including the ones you import, is the **Browse Mode**. Here, under Appearance > Editor, you can find all sorts of amazing options, from templates to template parts – which we will go through later – and patterns. Let's focus on patterns for now, as this interface really takes us to the next level once we start talking about adding our own and the types of patterns. Let's look at what patterns look like when we view all of them. In this screenshot, you can see them all loaded in the browser. The **All patterns** section is selected.

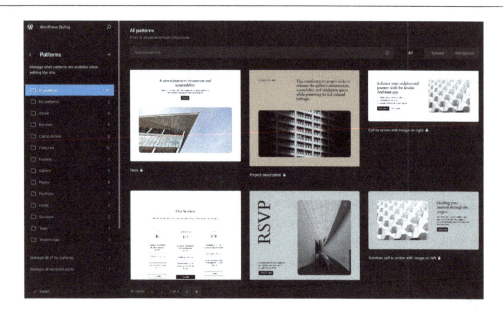

Figure 6.10 – The newer pattern browsing interface

This interface has a few different stages. *Figure 6.10* shows how you view all the added patterns. You can then go into **My patterns** to see just the ones you have created and shared on the site.

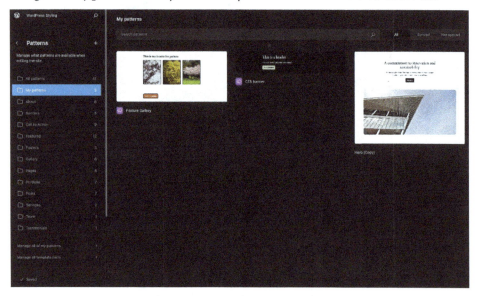

Figure 6.11 – Showing My patterns, which are ones you've added

This is a great way to see everything lined up and have further actions you can do such as import, duplicate, and others. From here, you can also go even further to view a single pattern view. Let's do that in the next screenshot.

Clicking in from the preceding state gives you a menu, which is behind the pencil icon in the following screenshot. This has a range of options, from duplicating the pattern to exporting JSON. This creates a downloadable file you can then import to another install. Pretty cool, right? We've shown how you can simply copy and paste, but this is another great option.

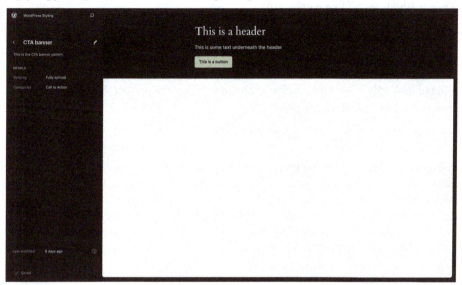

Figure 6.12 – Showing a single view of a pattern you've added

Clicking through, you can see the pattern's interface, which gives you the ability to change the categories. This allows you to really find out more, as you can see. Click one more time to get to the following screen.

Figure 6.13 – A single pattern view with the ability to edit

From *Figure 6.13*, you can see you can edit **PATTERN CATEGORIES**. This is a great way to manage your patterns.

We have discovered a lot so far, learning how to share patterns. Now we are going to move on to how you can create and share them in a theme.

Creating your own patterns and sharing in a theme

We are going to build on that by looking at how you package up patterns within themes. This is taking a pattern and making it automatically available to anyone that uses that theme – how cool is that?

There are two methods for adding patterns to your theme:

- Create a folder under your theme called `patterns/` and simply add them to it.
- Use `register_block_pattern()`, which is PHP.

We are going to look at how Twenty Twenty-Three implements the first method of creating a folder in a theme if you are using a block theme.

> **Note**
>
> A warning about what we are going to do next. We are going to be viewing the theme itself and the theme's code. It is never recommended to edit a default theme's code. In later chapters, we will look at how you can create your own theme and not change the theme files. The biggest reason to not edit these files is to ensure default themes can be easily updated in the future. If possible, open this within a code editor of your choice, but as we aren't teaching you about code in this book, you might not have one yet.

If you open the theme under `theme > edit`, you can see the following:

Figure 6.14 – The theme editor view with a pattern

Notice how there is a `patterns` folder and there are some patterns included? You can create this folder in your theme. You can then can create the patterns in the editor or you can create them in directly in the code. Let's have a look at some of the heading details you need to include:

```
/**
 * Title: Call to action
 * Slug: twentytwentythree/cta
 * Categories: featured
 * Keywords: Call to action
 * Block Types: core/buttons
 */
```

Let's walk through what those values mean together:

- **Title**: What the pattern is called
- **Slug**: The theme/unique name
- **Categories**: Places you will find the pattern

There are optional settings you can add, but having those as basic ones is a great start. For example, you can even turn off visibility. You can learn more about block patterns here: `https://developer.wordpress.org/themes/advanced-topics/block-patterns/`. To explore the full list of categories you can find out more here: `https://developer.wordpress.org/themes/features/block-patterns/#pattern-categories`.

Now we know how to add a pattern to a theme and have learned a lot more about patterns. Let's move on to level up our knowledge about patterns by learning about synced patterns.

Reusable blocks and synced patterns

Patterns are great, but even more useful are patterns that you can edit and reuse. Historically, there was a concept called **reusable blocks**. This is mentioned as you will probably find many mentions in the documentation for this. Synced patterns are the term commonly used now and was coined on purpose to clarify the use.

What are synced patterns?

Let's start by creating a synced pattern from a new pattern:

1. We have a pattern that is a heading, a gallery with some duotone styling, and also a call-to-action button. As you can see here, we are then going to create it into a pattern.

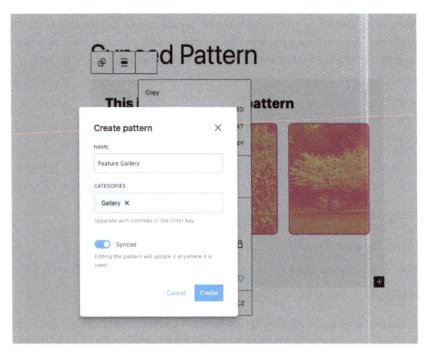

Figure 6.15 –The Create pattern modal with Synced on

Don't forget to add the categories and ensure that the **Synced** option is on, because that is what we are going to do. It typically is on by default.

2. That is all you have to do to create a synced pattern but what does it mean and how is it an advantage? You can see the unique coloring now in the view in this screenshot.

Figure 6.16 – A synced pattern in list view

Opening that up shows that everything is still there, but you can now use this pattern in another post. Let's do just that.

3. Open another post, after publishing the last one and search for your new pattern. Then add it. Look at that! You have the same pattern but in a different post! Pretty cool. Now, let's go back to the pattern and perhaps edit the duotone to be mono. What do you think will happen? Will all instances change? Yes, that's right! Because we have a synced pattern, you'll now see all changes will sync – how cool! Any change made in any post or page where a synced pattern is used will update instantly.

In the next screenshot, we can see the pattern that we've been working on together previewed.

Figure 6.17 – Previewing the synced pattern

As you can see, with a simple change the pattern is changed everywhere you need it.

Now we have a synced pattern, let's consider how we could take our knowledge even further by detaching or undoing a pattern.

Detaching a pattern

Syncing is great, but sometimes you might want to detach a pattern to just have an instance that is different. You can do this easily using **Detach**.

Let's first open the pattern in the post, then click the toolbar, select the menu icon for more and open the dropdown, then select **Detach**, as you can see in the screenshot.

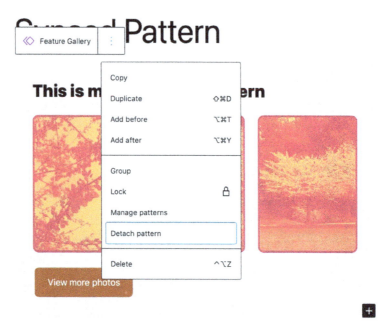

Figure 6.18 – Detach settings for a pattern

What this does is open the styling and free it from other instances of the pattern. You can now edit it and it won't impact any others. Think of it as a new pattern on its own now. You can see the editing styling is now open in the following screenshot.

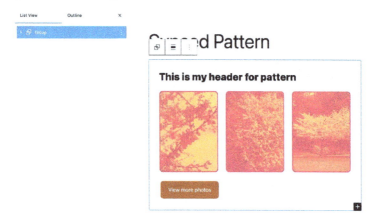

Figure 6.19 – A detached pattern

This is a great way of being able to take a pattern and customize it in just one instance you need, without impacting all cases.

Patterns that sync are incredibly powerful. Let's learn more in our discovery of patterns by learning next about the reusable interface.

Using the reusable blocks section for patterns

The interface for **reusable blocks** has been repurposed for patterns. You can find it under **Manage all my patterns**.

Figure 6.20 – Manage all of my patterns

Once you are within this section, you can then either import or add a new pattern.

The same goes for the JSON file uploading that exists within this interface.

Figure 6.21 – JSON import for patterns

Importing JSON in this section could change as versions are updated. However, importing JSON is a great way, in this and other sections, to update patterns. To do this, you simply click **Import from JSON** and you can upload the file.

This interface concludes our journey around patterns. We have learned so much and now we have even imported JSON files. Let's finish with a summary of everything we have learned together.

Summary

In this chapter, we took our understanding of patterns to a practical level by learning not only how to create them but even syncing them and beyond.

Let's recap what we have explored in this chapter:

- We have learned to create a pattern using the editor interface.
- We learned how patterns are added to themes using folders.
- We learned what a synced pattern is and how to create one.
- We learned how to detach a synced pattern.
- We learned about the **My patterns** interface and how we can share patterns.

Next, we are going to explore how you can discover more patterns through the WordPress pattern directory and use a whole range of pre-built patterns created by others. This opens up even more possibilities for you to create perfect content.

Questions

Answer the following questions to test your knowledge of this chapter:

1. Most patterns start with a container block. Is this statement true or false?

    a. True

    b. False

2. Define a synced pattern.

    a. Patterns you can make changes to by editing and the changes are then reflected across all instances of that pattern.

    b. Patterns that are locked and you are only able to make changes by removing them.

3. The term for un-syncing a pattern is:

    a. Unhook

    b. Unsync

c. Detach

Answers

1. Most patterns start with a container block. Is this statement true?

   a. True

2. Define a synced pattern.

   a. Patterns you can make changes to by editing and the changes are then reflected across all instances of that pattern.

3. The term for unsyncing a pattern is:

   c. Detach

Further reading

Discover more about block patterns by looking here:

`https://learn.wordpress.org/workshop/intro-to-block-patterns/`

7
Discovering the WordPress Pattern Directory

In the previous chapter, we looked at how you can create your own patterns. While that is great, there is a directory of incredible patterns that users across the community of WordPress have created. This is known as the WordPress Pattern Directory. It hosts an incredible array of patterns ready to use in whatever way you want.

In this chapter, we will discover the following together:

- What is the WordPress Pattern Directory?
- Finding and using a pattern
- Adding your own pattern

We will then close with a summary of the **Pattern Directory** as we move to close this section exploring WordPress patterns.

What is the WordPress Pattern Directory?

The **WordPress Pattern Directory**, often referred to as the **Block Pattern Directory**, can be found at https://wordpress.org/patterns/. This is an incredible resource for anyone looking to not only save time by using patterns, but also find that perfect fit visually.

The Directory went live in July 2021 as part of the **WordPress 5.8** release, with a smaller set of community-created patterns that are shown by default. Should you want to see all the patterns you can do so by changing the dropdown on the main toolbar of the Pattern Directory from **Curated** to **Community**. Since its launch, it has grown to hold a wide range of patterns to enable you to find literally whatever you want.

Once you go to the **Pattern Directory**, you are welcomed with a range of options as you can see in *Figure 7.1*.

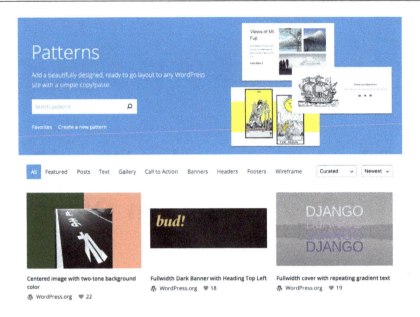

Figure 7.1 – The WordPress Pattern Directory front page

Within the Directory, you can do a range of things, including search and filter by category to your favorite patterns so that you can come back to them later.

There is also a **Featured** section, shown in the following screenshot, that offers a great way to view selected patterns.

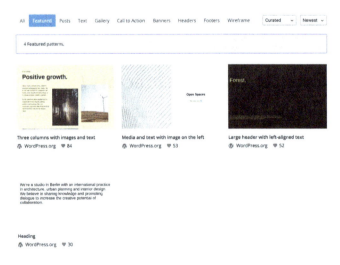

Figure 7.2 – Featured patterns shown in the Directory

To mark a pattern as a favorite and upload your own patterns, you will need a `WordPress.org` account. You can discover more about that here: `https://login.wordpress.org/register`.

Now, let's move on together to learn about using patterns directly from the Directory.

Finding and using a pattern

Now that we know about the **Pattern Directory**, how do we use a pattern from it? There are a few methods. First, let's see how to search using the filters and getting the patterns for use on our sites.

Using the Pattern Directory itself

Imagine you want to find a gallery pattern. Let's do that together by finding one that exists within the **Pattern Directory**:

1. First, visit the **Pattern Directory** and filter by **Gallery**. You should see a number of different **Gallery** patterns, as shown in this screenshot.

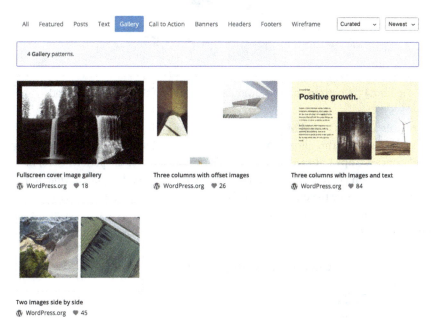

Figure 7.3 – The Gallery patterns

2. As you can see in the preceding screenshot, each of these patterns has some information displayed, including how many times they have been marked as favorites and a brief description, along with a thumbnail image.

3. Next, let's click on the pattern named **Three columns with images and text**. This pattern has been marked as a favorite more than any other pattern. Let's discover more about this pattern. As you can see in *Figure 7.4*, selecting the pattern takes you to its dedicated page.

Figure 7.4 – A pattern's page showing all the details of that pattern selected

4. It also reveals a section called **More from this designer** that showcases other patterns created by the same designer. This allows you to explore other patterns they have made. In *Figure 7.5*, you will notice a **Copy Pattern** button. You can click that to get the pattern code. Let's do that right now. Click on the button. While it seems like nothing has happened, what it has done is copied the pattern code to your clipboard. If you were to then go to a text file, for example, you could paste the output. You should see a success message once you have clicked **Copy Pattern**, as shown in *Figure 7.5*.

Figure 7.5 – Copying a pattern

This means you have got the pattern and now you can add it to your site. Let's do that now.

It is important to keep in mind that **Copy Pattern** is not the only way to get the pattern code. There is a quicker method and that's to grab the code right from the grid view with the relevant **Copy** button, as shown in the following screenshot.

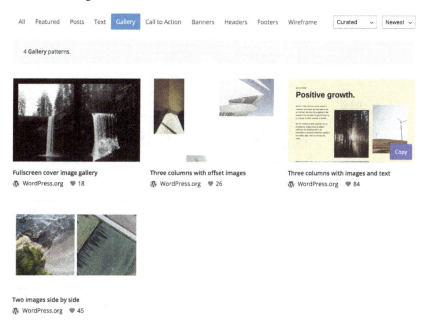

Figure 7.6 – Copying a pattern directly from the grid view

This allows you to grab the code right then and there without even having to go into the pattern itself – how cool is that? All you need to do is click **Copy** and then you can take that right into the editor. Let's try that:

Having copied the pattern, go to the site you want to add the pattern to and go into a post or page. I am using a simple post already set up that I want to add a gallery to. This pattern will look great there. Add a new line to form a space within the editor – this will help you find the right spot. Then, paste using either the keyboard or whatever mouse combination works for your operating system. You should see something similar to what is shown in *Figure 7.7*.

Figure 7.7 – Adding a pattern

That's amazing, right? You just grabbed the code from the Directory and put it straight into your site. Now, the pattern is live, and you can click and edit anything you want. I am going to click and change the title and some images. Let's see what that looks like.

If you want to see the code you can do so by clicking **Code editor** under the options within the editor sidebar, as seen in *Figure 7.8*.

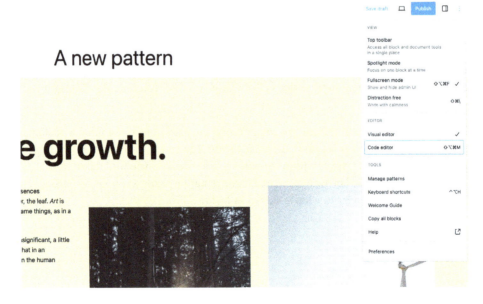

Figure 7.8 – The Code editor option

You can copy patterns through the **Code editor** by selecting and then copying all the blocks. This is useful if you want to then bring them into your theme files or share the code.

Next, use **Replace** to change the images for the different ones and make this your own pattern. For this example, we are going to also edit the images using the "Crop" tool. It's handy to resize images and is available under the Image block toolbar.

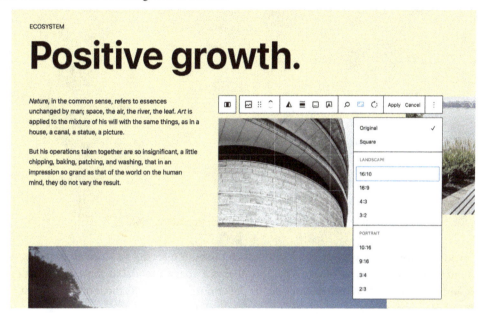

Figure 7.9 – The pattern changes

You can now view the pattern using preview and see your changes on the front-end of the site. We just experienced how easy it is to copy a pattern from the **Pattern Directory**. But, it is also possible to find patterns within the editor itself. Let's explore how to find patterns within the editor.

Finding patterns within the editor

The ability to search the Directory is great. You can easily browse and find things, but there is nothing quite like finding things right where you need them. That's why having access to the **Pattern Directory** inside the editor is really powerful and probably the most likely place you are going to use it.

There are two viewing options, the side panel navigation and the modal browser. The side panel is more limited, while the newer modal browser gives you more of the full Directory view. This time let's use the Twenty Twenty-Four theme so we can see some different patterns in the browser.

See *Figure 7.10* for the Pattern Directory in the side panel. You can reach this by selecting + from the toolbar and then **Patterns**. By default, it selects **Blocks**.

Figure 7.10 – Adding a pattern from the side section

Before we go into the next step, let's pause and notice the button saying **Explore all patterns**. We are going to click that in the next stage. What this does is it opens a modal to show all the patterns available and we already discovered that in *Chapter 5*. For now, though, let's focus on adding just one using the interface we see first.

Once you see the interface in the preceding screenshot, you can simply click on any section and see the relevant patterns. For example, if you selected **Text**, you would see the following:

Figure 7.11 – A pattern selected and added to the editor

This shows all the text patterns available, including those in the theme. Simply clicking a pattern adds it as seen in *Figure 7.11*. You even get a confirmation message as the pattern is added to your content.

> **Note**
>
> It's worth noting that the current theme's patterns show first (if any are assigned to the selected category), allowing you to add those more easily.

Let's click **Explore all patterns** now to access them all. Once you have clicked to view all patterns you are taken to see the modal shown in *Figure 7.12* where you can view them all.

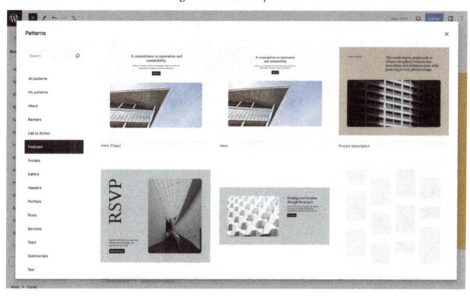

Figure 7.12 – Browsing patterns in the editor using the modal experience

The modal view is really nice to browse as it's clear, focused, allows easy browsing, and helps you find just that perfectly fitting pattern. Let's find a banner for our content now:

1. While viewing all patterns, click on **Banners**. You will see a full-screen view of all the banners available to you, both from your current theme and on the **Pattern Directory**.

2. Click the banner pattern you want to add, and it will be added right into your content as you can see in *Figure 7.13*.

Figure 7.13 – A banner pattern added to the editor

It really is that simple to work with patterns and because each one can be edited, you then get the benefit of all the styling available through design tools and the editor. In this heavily styled banner, you could, for example, change the images and inherit the styling applied to them. You can see this in *Figure 7.14*.

Figure 7.14 – Swapped-out images in an existing pattern

The duotone effect was retained when I added new images through the **Replace** option in the image block toolbar. This is pretty cool as it means the new images fit right in and I don't have to do anything to keep the style.

Patterns are truly powerful in their portability and ability to adapt their style once added or keep a pre-configured style..

We have finished our exploration of finding and using patterns from the Directory. Let's now look at how we can add our own patterns to the Directory to give something back.

Adding your own pattern

You can add your own pattern to the Directory. This is a great way to share your creations and play a part in the community. Before you do this, though, there are some guidelines you should review that you can find here: `https://wordpress.org/patterns/about/`. These guidelines include things such as ensuring no self-promotion.

Let's get started:

1. Log in to your `WordPress.org` account.

2. Once you have logged in, click on **New Pattern** and you will see an interface similar to that shown in *Figure 7.15*. if you have clicked on 'New Pattern' once logged in. From here, you can create your pattern to be added to the Directory. You can create within this interface or simply copy your pattern in from elsewhere – let's explore that now.

Figure 7.15 – The interface to add your own pattern

3. Remember from the previous chapter how you can simply copy and paste patterns? You can do that here too – yes, it works across any installation! Give it a try!

4. Once you have added your pattern, you can publish it and the pattern review team will consider it for publication.

If you have patterns added, they will show as a list on your profile. This is a great thing for contributors.

Summary

In this chapter, we took our knowledge of patterns further by discovering the WordPress **Pattern Directory** together. With this new knowledge, we now have access to more patterns and can boost our content.

Let's recap what we can now do after our exploration:

- We learned what the WordPress **Pattern Directory** is.
- We discovered how to find a pattern.
- We learned how to use a pattern from the **Pattern Directory**.
- We discovered how to add our own patterns to the **Pattern Directory**.

Now that we have this knowledge, we are now going to move on in the next chapter to wrap up our exploration of patterns. We will review some inspiration for creating patterns and finally look at what comes next as we go further in our journey together.

Questions

Answer the following questions to test your understanding of this chapter:

1. What is the WordPress **Pattern Directory**?

   a. A paid service you go to buy patterns from.

   b. A free Directory you can get patterns from.

2. You can copy and paste a pattern. True or false?

   a. False

   b. True

3. You can't style patterns once you've copied them from the **Pattern Directory**. True or false?

   a. True

   b. False

Answers

1. What is the WordPress **Pattern Directory**?

   b. A free Directory you can get patterns from.

2. You can copy and paste a pattern. True or false?

   b. True

3. You can't style patterns once you've copied them from the **Pattern Directory**. True or false?

   b. False

Further reading

Block Pattern Directory: `https://wordpress.org/documentation/article/block-pattern-directory/`

8

Wrapping Up Patterns

Our previous chapters have led us on a discovery path that has taken us through learning what patterns are, how to use them, and where to find them. In this final chapter on patterns, we are going to explore how to get inspiration to fuel our pattern creation. This chapter will guide you to find that inspiration and give you a glimpse of how patterns can be really fun to create. Then we are going to look at how you can add not just core blocks but also add other blocks into patterns, and let your creativity soar!

In this chapter, we will discover the following together:

- Let's get creative – inspiring patterns
- Finding inspiration
- Combining beyond core blocks

We will then close with a summary as we look to move on from patterns into the next chapter on templates, starting to discover what site editing is. It's going to be an exciting journey as we move up from just looking at blocks, past patterns, to template parts, templates, and the site itself.

Let's get creative – inspiring patterns

We are going to look a little later in this chapter at where you can go to find inspiration, but for now let's look at some inspiring patterns that show how far you can take the patterns themselves. Some come from the Pattern Directory and some from the Museum of Block Art.

The **Museum of Block Art (MOBA)** is a great source of inspiration as you can browse so many incredible art-like creations. Please refer to this link for more detail: `https://block-museum.com/`. The MOBA has some incredible examples to show. Let's look at a few here that show how patterns and blocks can be art.

The following one shown in *Figure 8.1* is by Mel Choyce-Dwan, a designer who contributes a lot to WordPress and takes the concept of block art literally by creating a block composition.

Figure 8.1 – Block Composition by Mel Choyce-Dwan

As stated in the description, this was created using the Columns block, Group block, and Spacer block. You can explore more of the code in each block within the museum by viewing the individual links: `https://block-museum.com/2022/01/11/block-composition/`.

The example in *Figure 8.2*, called *Golden Ratio*, is a truly impressive pattern using just a few blocks.

Figure 8.2 – Golden Ratio by Tetsuaki Hamano

Figure 8.3 can be explored more here: `https://block-museum.com/2022/04/19/golden-ratio/`

If traditional Gallery blocks are boring you, Anne McCarthy, another contributor to WordPress and the museum, has you covered with an incredible pattern.

Figure 8.3 – Shining through by Anne McCarthy

Exploring the code truly shows how combining simple effects with the Gallery block unlocks its potential: `https://block-museum.com/2022/12/26/shining-through/`

As we reach the end of our journey through the museum, let's close with one final example by Rich Tabor.

Figure 8.4 – The Equinoctial Tide by Rich Tabor

To explore this styling further, visit this link: `https://block-museum.com/2022/01/11/the-equinoctial-tide/`.

As you can see, simple patterns can once you start experimenting easily create art forms. All it takes are 2-3 simple block combinations and some design tools, plus a little bit of imagination, and you too could send your block to the museum. It is open for contributions: `https://block-museum.com/contribute/`.

In the spirit of encouraging, you to create your own patterns, *Figure 8.5* shows a recent contribution I made based on the default theme Twenty Twenty.

Figure 8.5 – Twenty Twenty

The following link will take you to the Twenty Twenty theme: `https://block-museum.com/2023/07/25/twenty-twenty/`

The preceding pattern takes inspiration from the default theme Twenty Twenty for WordPress. This hasn't so much practical application as it shows what could be possible when combining these elements.

Furthermore, in my own explorations within a little project called Patterninspiration, (`http://patternspiration.com/`) this site features a range of patterns created, as shown in the following figure.

Figure 8.6 – Patternspiration pattern

These artistic experiments might seem fun, but there is also a very practical aspect to them. You are learning the boundaries and features of patterns and the workings of the editor by exploring.

One thing to note about patterns like the preceding is that while they might look amazing in one browser at an exact size, once you change the width they might not. Therefore, it's important to test across all sizes of screens. That's both the beauty and issue with using patterns to create these pieces.

While the preceding examples take it a little further into the conceptual realm to see would be achieved visually, if you want something both practical and beautiful, there are some stunning examples in the **Pattern Directory**. For example, the following shows how you must be careful to be accessible when using text. It looks pretty good in the following screenshot:

Figure 8.7 – Django pattern

You can find this pattern here: `https://wordpress.org/patterns/pattern/fullwidth-cover-with-repeating-gradient-text/`. There's a lot going on here to unpack, and that's cool. However, as the following screenshot shows, there is a warning in the sidebar about color and accessibility issues. You need to be careful when creating things that use text to avoid these issues. If you are going to use something on a site, balancing art and function is key.

Figure 8.8 – Showing accessibility issues with Django text

The following example, "Let 'em Roll," is great to demonstrate how text can be both artistic and adaptable to different screen sizes. As shown in *Figure 8.9*, in the **Pattern Directory** you can use the dropdown and select different widths of viewports.

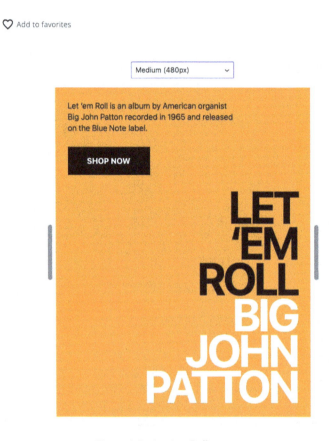

Figure 8.9 – Let 'em Roll pattern

Looking around the editor, we can see how this pattern is made, as shown in *Figure 8.10*.

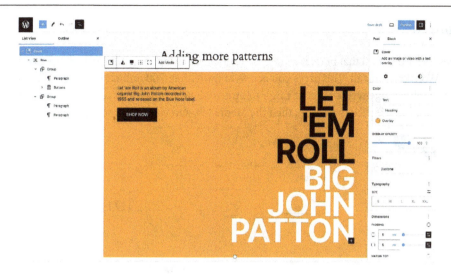

Figure 8.10 – Showing the formatting of the "Let 'em Roll" pattern

This is a simple matter of groups and design tools, but when combined they build up into this impactful banner.

We've explored a lot so far, having now discovered some new patterns along with how they work. Let's move on to find inspiration and unleash our creativity even further.

Finding inspiration

When considering inspiration for patterns, it's useful to start thinking about what could or should be turned into a pattern – for instance, something you might want to reuse across multiple areas of the site, or across even multiple sites. Some good examples include testimonials, contact strips, and call-for-action banners.

You can get inspiration from anywhere – think about real sites, the ones you use daily, and the common patterns those have.

One thing you need inspiration for is the images and content for your site. This is where services like Openverse come in handy, offering a portal to easily get resources with licenses that allow free use.

Openverse

Sometimes it's hard to find that perfect image. You can search using something called **Openverse** right from your WordPress install. This gives you access to more than 700 million creative works. You can discover more about **Openverse** here: `https://openverse.org/`. To access the service right from your dashboard, simply click the + icon, then the **Media** tab, and you'll see a section called **Openverse**.

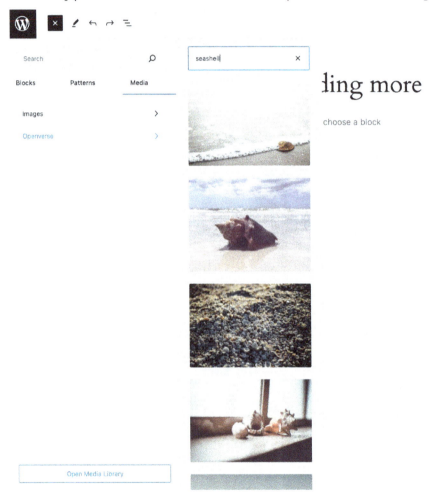

Figure 8.11 – Openverse in the editor interface

In *Figure 8.11*, you can see the interface for Openverse within the editor. This is an incredibly convenient way of accessing content with which to embellish your site.

Pattern Directory

The **Pattern Directory** has a lot more inspiration than just the categories you can browse through. It has a range of further options to explore, including curated designs and much more. Let's look at a few of these options together.

Curated and wireframe patterns

As mentioned, you can find much more than just full patterns on the **Pattern Directory** – there are also amazing wireframes for you to explore. These are great if you want something that gives you a starting point without any design of your own and build from there. You can access the **wireframes**, from the Wireframes link in the category navigation of the Pattern Directory. See *Figure 8.12*.

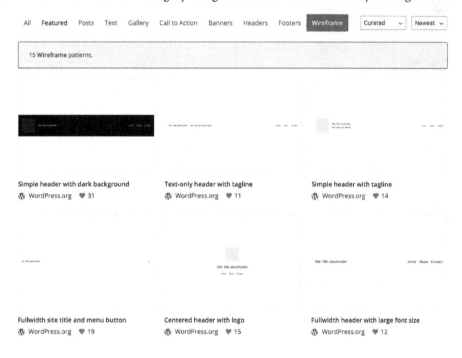

Figure 8.12 – Wireframe patterns

Once selected, you will see all the patterns that fall into this category. They are a great way to apply your own theme styling to a pattern or even go beyond that. Not having a style pre-applied to the pattern can often be a great way to start creating a simple theme.

The **Curated** option is for patterns that have been reviewed for quality. You can find these patterns by selecting the **Curated** filter from the dropdown next to the **Wireframe** button. This will populate the view with those types of patterns.

Community search

The **Pattern Directory** has a lot more potential than just finding patterns using simple tabs. There is also a newly available **Community** search function to explore countless community-created patterns. You can see these in the following screenshot, where we have selected **Community** from the same dropdown as **Curated** previously.

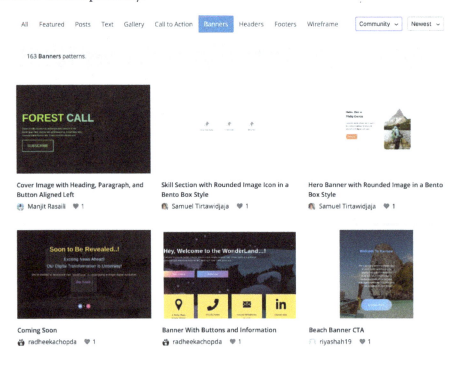

Figure 8.13 – Banners created by the community in the Pattern Directory

Once you select the **Community** option, the display pre-fills with a range of different patterns depending on the options you have selected in the tabs. You can find so many more patterns this way.

Default theme inspiration

Each year WordPress releases a new default theme, the most recent being **Twenty Twenty-Four** as of writing this book. These typically have lots of inspiration for patterns and much more besides, including best practices for implementation. You can see some examples from Twenty Twenty-Four in the following screenshot.

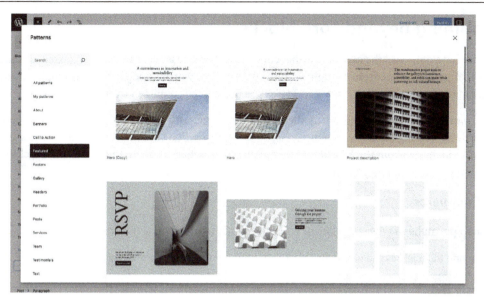

Figure 8.14 – Patterns from Twenty Twenty-Four theme

These patterns are a great starting point to take and then customize however you want. It's particularly easy to do this, as patterns are open to easy adaption. You could also use them simply as fuel for inspiration.

It's also good to go back over default themes from the past for inspiration and even look at the top themes in the WordPress theme directory. Load them up on a site and take inspiration as to what is possible with patterns.

Look at the real world

Nothing beats being inspired by real sites. Look at what common patterns are used. You could also consider looking at pattern and component sites for inspiration – there are many out there to consider.

The following are just a few resources for inspiration:

- `https://ui-patterns.com/`: This site has so many strong examples of interface patterns you can use.

- `https://designpatternsformentalhealth.org/`: Knowing what makes a pattern to support mental health can be useful across so many use cases, so this site is incredibly worth exploring, particularly the examples.

- `https://m3.material.io/components`: Google's team have some great component patterns to learn from.

Keeping your own screenshot collection of patterns as you journey around the web is a great way to start thinking about what could be useful. You could even start sketching possible combinations of blocks.

Combining beyond core blocks

So far, we have only used the core blocks that come with WordPress itself. We haven't looked at using blocks that perhaps come from a plugin within a pattern. It is worth noting that many plugins come with a range of patterns, either built in or via blocks that can be combined to create patterns.

It's also worth remembering that many themes already come with patterns as well. We've explored this a little by treating the default themes as a source of inspiration. This is true for paid themes and those you might get from the WordPress theme directory. Often, though, these use core blocks as their sources – so let's go beyond just those in our exploration now.

WooCommerce

This shop plugin has a range of patterns, which are ready to use upon activation.

You can find them just as you would any other pattern under the pattern browser, as shown in *Figure 8.15*.

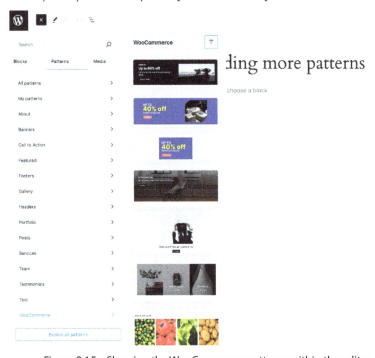

Figure 8.15 – Showing the WooCommerce patterns within the editor

Again, you can also click **Explore all patterns** or view this in all the usual ways we've examined previously. Some are dependent on certain pages, content, and flows to function, but they are great to get you started right away on your store design. You can of course combine Woo blocks to create your own or style them differently to give them some flair, as exhibited in the following screenshot.

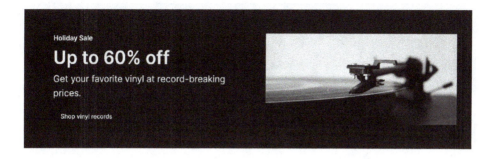

Figure 8.16 – A WooCommerce example block with some styling added

By using design tools, you can truly make this yours, as shown in the following example.

Figure 8.17 – Changing the styling on WooCommerce block

In this example, all that has been used are a range of borders, background colors, and simple text coloring. It combines to create more of a card-like look for a shop's holiday sale.

Jetpack

Jetpack also has some core blocks that can be used in patterns. Jetpack is a plugin that not only helps you manage your site, but also comes with a range of blocks that boost your site.

In the following example, I have taken a simple **Group** block and added that around the business hours block to create a reusable business opening-hours pattern. There is a border, with a 6px rounding and simple background color.

Figure 8.18 – An example opening hours pattern from Jetpack

All you have to do is select **Create pattern** using the block toolbar and you can then share and reuse it as you wish. Jetpack has a range of useful blocks like this to create frequently used patterns and commonly expected functionality for your site.

Summary

Patterns are truly powerful and while blocks are incredible, this chapter has shown that when most people plan to create a site, they think in terms of patterns, not single blocks. This is why working and learning to make patterns is a skill that will unlock so much more for you and your content going forward.

Let's recap what we have covered in our exploration together in this chapter:

- We learned that patterns can be art and viewed some incredible examples of that.

- We learned that whilst artistic patterns are great, if we are creating content for actual use, we need to consider accessibility and how someone might use our pattern.

- We discovered where to go to find inspiration for patterns.

- We learned that it's not just core blocks that can be used in patterns; through patterns we have access to many themes and plugins.

Now we have all this knowledge about patterns, let's move on to template parts, templates, and the site itself. It's going to be an exciting journey that will see us learning about site editing and a brand-new interface.

Questions

Answer the following questions to test your understanding of this chapter:

1. What is the MOBA or Museum of Block Art?

    a. It is an online resource to view block art and get inspiration.

    b. A physical museum of blocks.

2. WordPress has a built-in color accessibility checker for block text. True or false?

    a. False

    b. True

3. What is Openverse?

    a. An online poetry service.

    b. A space online where you can browse more than 700 million creative works.

4. You can't use blocks that are from plugins such as WooCommere within patterns. True or false?

    a. True

    b. False

Answers

1. What is the MOBA or Museum of Block Art?

    a. It is an online resource to view block art and get inspiration.

2. WordPress has a built-in color accessibility checker for block text. True or false?

    b. True

3. What is Openverse?

    b. A space online where you can browse more than 700 million creative works.

4. You can't use blocks that are from plugins such as WooCommere within patterns. True or false?

    b. False

Part 3:
Template Parts and Templates

Template parts and templates come together to wrap around patterns and blocks, styling your site's content. In this part, you will discover the Site Editor and learn how to use its features.

This section has the following chapters:

- *Chapter 9, An Introduction to Site Editing*
- *Chapter 10, Discovering and Creating Template Parts*
- *Chapter 11, Discovering and Creating Templates*
- *Chapter 12, Templates Wrap-Up*

An Introduction to Site Editing

We are going to dive into some more advanced concepts as we begin to look at templates. Before we look at templates, we need to pause to review the interface of the Site Editor and unlock its potential. In previous chapters, we looked at how you can use the editor, also called the Block Editor, to create content. Now we are going beyond the area we think of as content and onto the entire site. In this chapter, we will discover the following together:

- What is site editing?
- Concepts: template parts and templates
- A quick guide to the interface
- Site blocks
- Design tools in site editing

Once we have covered the basics of site editing, we are going to discuss each element that makes up a site, from template parts through to templates, and see how we can create each of them together.

What is site editing?

You may have heard it being called **full site editing** or **customization** recently; it all means the same thing, that you are using an editor to edit your entire site. This includes editing sitewide elements like headers, footers, navigation and even site logos.

Support for this new feature was first added in WordPress version 5.9 with the release called Josephine in January 2022. Additional features have been added in multiple releases as this feature has been iterated on and improved.

Those of you who are familiar with other page builders might instantly recognize the interface of the WordPress Site Editor. It has a lot of familiar concepts. It also doesn't stray too far from the editor we have been using so far. There are a few more options to it, though. We will discover what they are a little later when we walk through the interface.

You might be wondering why should WordPress have a site editing feature?

Previously, you would have been limited within a theme to either content areas or widget areas that the theme allows you to work within. This limited the scope for the creation of both themes and content.

While site builders have come onto the market, the need for WordPress to provide more flexibility for those creating themes and content was clear. This is the root of the reason why site editing was created. It isn't meant to be a fully-fledged page builder; in many ways, it is a starting point, and you will find a lot of plugins and builders have taken that and built even more incredible experiences using it.

Let's now move on to exploring beyond the interface and looking at some of the concepts you will discover within site editing: template parts and templates.

Exploring template parts and templates

There are two key concepts that need to be mentioned, templates and template parts:

- **Template parts**: Reusable pieces that go across your site. A good example of these are headers or footers.
- **Templates**: Pre-set entire layouts that are more than just patterns. A good example of this is a front page or a particular archive page layout.

These two concepts form the foundation for interactions within the Site Editor, as we'll discover. In a later chapter, we will combine this with global styling to truly unlock its power. There is a lot you can do with the Site Editor, and it can be overwhelming. The best approach is to learn task by task. So, let's do just that and break it down into more familiar concepts.

A quick guide to the interface

As noted, if you look at the editor, it is similar to many page and site builders. However, let's take a walkthrough of some of the key pages and areas to see what is available.

If you have a block theme installed, you can reach the Site Editor from the section shown within the following screenshot. An example of this is the default theme Twenty Twenty-Four. This editor can be found under **Appearance** by selecting **Editor**, as you can see in *Figure 9.1*.

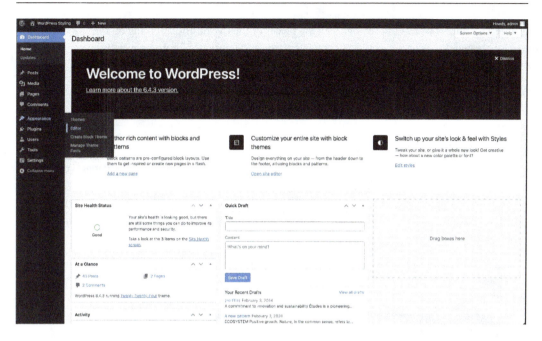

Figure 9.1 – Showing how to get to the Editor in the menu

Once you have followed the path shown in *Figure 9.1*, you will be able to view the interface of the editor for the site. As you can see, in *Figure 9.2*, it's quite a different interface to the one you get from when you add or edit a post or page.

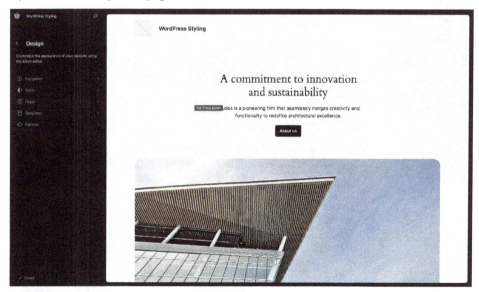

Figure 9.2 – The first screen you see when you click Editor, also known as Browse Mode

This interface allows you to interact with all the pieces of the theme and anything on the site that you have also created, for example, patterns, template parts, and templates. From here, you can even create new versions of these types and new styling.

You will notice a new interface pattern emerging from the left sidebar as a menu for sections you click on. This sidebar holds useful information and is wider so it can accommodate all different types using the same layout.

As you click into the screens, you typically get an overview or browsing interface – you will remember we covered some of this in Chapter 5 when we explored patterns. If you click on Pages, you get a list of all pages. Now, let's go back and look at Templates. Click a template that says "page". It's often confusing what is a template, and we're going to discuss this more as we progress. For now, you should know that your home page is indeed a theme template. The content you create is either in the form of pages or posts.

Go back to the list before we clicked on **Pages**. Click on **Templates**. Then select one, for example, **Blog Home** if you're using the Twenty Twenty-Four theme. As you can see in *Figure 9.3*, you get a summary page.

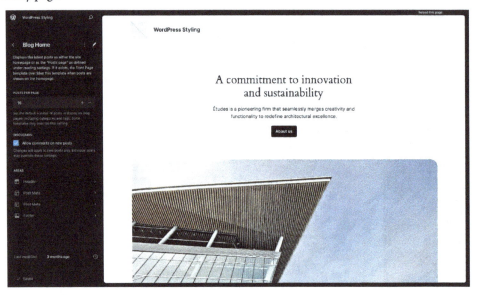

Figure 9.3 – The details of a template page

This is a great way to not only be able to adjust settings but also see the template and what you have for the page itself. Each **Area** is a part you can go into and discover further. For example, let's click **Header**.

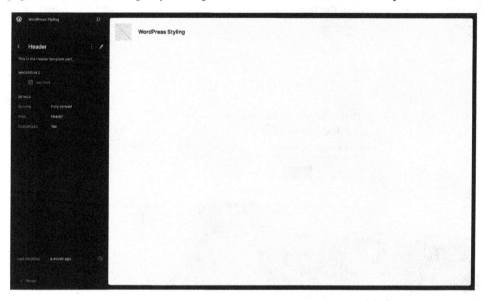

Figure 9.4 – The details for a template part

Here, you can see the **Header** is now being shown with everything it contains. Notice that the little pencil edit icon visible on all screens? That is how you go into the editing interface out of browsing mode and can start to interact more.

Before we go into the editor, one of the best pages in this browsing view is **Templates**, as this shows you every single template and allows you rapid access. Similarly, you can do this for navigation elements. This first view is useful as a check of your site.

Anything changed in Templates will be removed once you change the theme – this is called being specific to it. With pages, what is removed depends on the content and the template – so the content stays even if you change the theme. This can be a little confusing, but once you start creating your site it will become clear.

Let's now move into the editor itself. We're going to go up a level, pick a template – for example, **Blog Home** – and then click on the pencil icon. In the following screenshot, you can see the Site Editor with the side panel open showing the template.

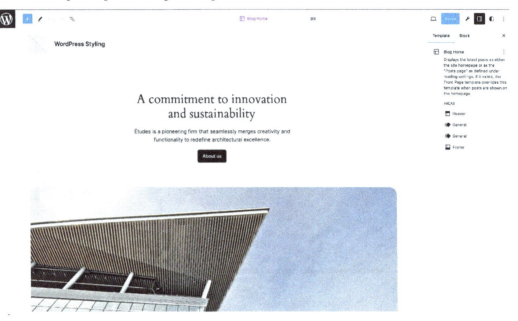

Figure 9.5 – The Site Editor screen with the side panel open

This interface has some similarities with the post and page editor. We can see the top toolbar. Notice that the sidebar is the same. The actions translate, but there are some key elements that are worth talking about.

The central section in the top toolbar has a handy link to something called **Command Palette**. This has a range of commands that you can use to quickly go anywhere. Let's try typing Pattern and see what we get. You can also access this using *Cmd + K* or the equivalent for your system.

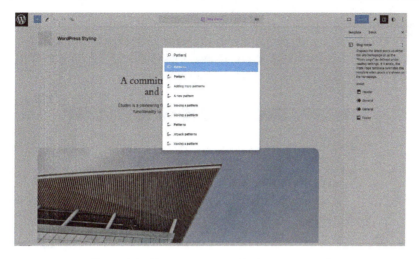

Figure 9.6 – Showing command palette activated

If you wanted to click any of these you would get taken to that link, for example **Making a pattern** guide, or **Patterns**. It's a great rapid way of working and is growing in usability across WordPress. Due to the complexity of the editor here, learning commands such as this comes in handy.

Let's move past this though and look at how this interface is a little different from the one we know. This sidebar seems a bit different, and there are a few new toolbar icons to explore. The first new icon is **Styles** (the circle that is half black, half white). This was previously known as **Global Styles**. In simple terms, think of this as your site's entire styling, not just per template or per block.

Let's now look at what the side panel displays when the styles are open, you can see that in the next image.

Figure 9.7 – Styles panel open

As you can see when the styles panel is open, it has its own sidebar, and you can go into each section. There is also a brand-new icon that you've not seen here called **Style Book.** This is the eye icon next to the **Styles** heading. This is incredibly handy, and we're going to explore styles and this in a later chapter. For now, let's just click and show you. See *Figure 9.8.*

Figure 9.8 – Style Book activated within the editor

This is a way of seeing all your styles laid out block by block. This is incredibly useful as you adjust the styles.

> **Note**
>
> You don't have to use everything available within the site editing functionality. You can even turn off certain features if you want to. We aren't going to be exploring this too much within this book, beyond looking at and the concept of theme.json. This file contains the theme settings that set the styling up for any theme.

Now we are going to move on to looking at site blocks. This reveals more of the power of the Site Editor by looking at specific blocks to use on our site.

Site blocks

When you use the Site Editor, there are specific blocks that are really useful when creating templates and template parts and thinking about sites. Let's look at just a few and, later on, we can go into more of them.

Spacer block

A key block when creating sites is the **spacer block**. This handy little block allows you to literally create just that – space between things. Let's look at how that might appear in a template. See *Figure 9.9*.

Figure 9.9 – The spacer block showing design tools

In the preceding screenshot, you can see the spacer block has a handy dot to move it and some simple interface tools in case you wish to change the size. Depending on the theme, you can set it to different values.

It's a good idea to be cautious about how many spacer blocks you add to a template as too many can become unmanageable at scale, but a few can really help with the layout and enable you to get just what you need.

Navigation block

Most sites need navigation, and you can add that to any header you want or template using the **navigation block**. Let's take a little look at this block. It's complex, but let's go over some of the key points. When we explore template parts, we're going to go further into this by looking at headers.

In this next screenshot, you can see the list view showing the navigation block. The settings for the block are also displayed in the side panel.

In this example, we are going to go to the Archive template. You can get to this in the same way we reached the previous template through the Editor browser. Under templates, select **All Archives**. Let's use this for the following example, as shown in *Figure 9.10*.

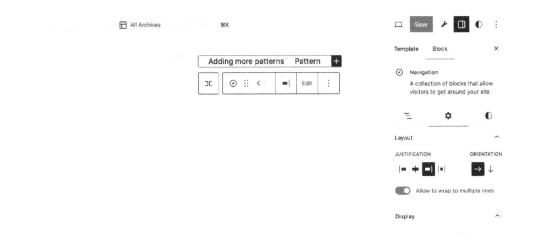

Figure 9.10 – Navigation block showing options in the side panel

The navigation block has the features most blocks have, but you can also set the mobile (hamburger) menu to be on just for mobiles, or always on. You can also choose what menu it displays. There are some quite in-depth design tools. In the next chapter, we are going to create a menu together.

Query loop block

The **Query Loop** block is a key block for site editing. This block loops through content, then outputs in a pattern you selected. We are going to initially have a light look at it, but we will explore it in more depth as we progress through the chapters together. There is a separate list view of menu items in the right sidebar next to the **Settings** and **Styles** tabs.

In *Figure 9.11*, you can see the query block with the side panel open showing the settings available to it.

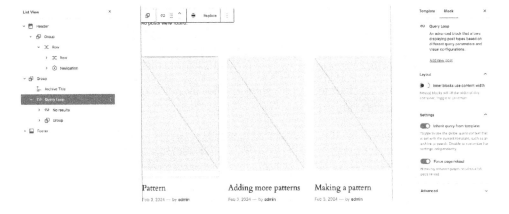

Figure 9.11 – Query block showing settings

As you can see in *Figure 9.11*, the query block also has some companion blocks, such as content, post title, comments, and many more. These are lockable and editable and allow you to have incredible control across what is locked.

We have learned a lot together in this section on site blocks. They are often quite complex, and we have only just started to discover their potential. Now, let's move on to discovering how design tools might work within site editing.

Design tools in site editing

There are specific design tools for site editing. Design tools can be within both the block and the Site Editor. In this section, we are going to explore them together.

Layout

This is essential when thinking of the entire template and site structure. You can break out sections or groups, or contain everything in your template. Let's look at how you can control things as a recap of something we saw on the **Group** block. See *Figure 9.12*.

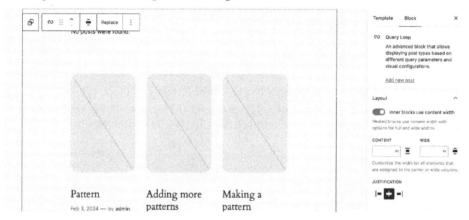

Figure 9.12 – Layout design tools on the group block

If you change the interface toggle to not use **Inner blocks use content width**, you can enter values. This means you are stating you don't want to use the default site width but create a custom one.

Sticky position

If you want an interesting effect for, say, a header, the sticky position which was added in WordPress 6.2 can be something to consider. **Sticky** means it sticks to the screen in a set position. You can find that in the position settings section, as shown in screenshot.

Figure 9.13 – Sticky position activated on the group block in the header template part

It is worth noting that you typically put the position on the group block not the template part to get the sticky effect. When working with effects such as this, exploring through experimentation is recommended as your theme might vary the results.

Dimensions – Fit, Fill, Fixed

Another design tool for dimensions on some blocks is the **Fit**, **Fill**, and **Fixed** options. This applies, for example, in *Figure 9.13*, to a heading's height. This isn't on all blocks, and more are being added all the time. It's important to check what functionality a block has before presuming what the block does.

Figure 9.14 – Dimension tools

This can give that control you might want for site-specific things to a level not previously available within the editor.

Summary

The Site Editor is a truly powerful tool, and we're only just starting to discover it in this chapter. As we begin to learn about each piece that goes together to create a site, from template parts to templates and even styles – we will start to unlock more and more of the potential together.

Let's recap what we now can do after exploring together:

- We discovered together what is site editing and why it's useful to have within WordPress.
- We learned about the interface differences and the new features there.
- We found out about some new blocks that help in creating site-specific content.
- We discovered design tools that also help with site editing.

This is all great foundational knowledge for us to start looking at each piece of the site that goes together. We're moving up past the block, past patterns, and into template parts first. Then we're going together to look at templates in this chapter – to finish our discovery of the structure of the site together.

Questions

Answer the following questions to test your knowledge of this chapter:

1. What is the definition of site editing?

   a. Editing the entire site not just the content inside.

   b. Editing just site headers and footers.

2. Which of these is a definition of a template part?

   a. Reusable pieces that go across your site. A good example of these are headers of footers.

   b. Reusable pieces that can be used on any content. Never headers or footers.

3. Which of these is a definition of a template?

   a. Pre-set entire layouts that are more than just patterns, for example, a front page or archive layout.

   b. Pre-set patterns are only grouped together into larger patterns.

4. Which of these were site blocks that we looked at in this chapter?

   a. Marquee block, rotation block, background block

   b. Spacer block, navigation block, query loop

Answers

1. What is the definition of site editing?

    a. Editing the entire site not just the content inside.

2. Which of these is a definition of a template part?

    a. Reusable pieces that go across your site. A good example of these are headers of footers.

3. Which of these is a definition of a template?

    a. Pre-set entire layouts that are more than just patterns, for example, a front page or archive layout.

4. Which of these were site blocks that we looked at in this chapter?

    b. Spacer block, navigation block, query loop

10

Discovering and Creating Template Parts

In previous chapters, we looked at blocks and then moved on to patterns. We also learned about the Site Editor. In this chapter, we are going to discover a new feature mentioned before: template parts.

Template parts are a collection of blocks made into a part that can be shared. You might be wondering what the difference is between this and a pattern. A template part is specifically used for structuring your site – for example, a header or a footer. There is even a specific section to browse and manage them within the Site Editor.

In this chapter, we will cover the following together:

- Creating a template part
- Using a template part
- Deleting a template part
- Detaching a template part
- Managing a template part

So, let's jump right in and discover the first part of this by creating a template part.

Creating a template part

As mentioned previously, template parts are part of the site's structure and are containers that contain other blocks. For example, they might be in the form of a group or column, or perhaps you have a site logo or navigation within a header. There are multiple ways of adding a template. Let's add one through Browse Mode first. Our walk-through here is a little longer than the previous ones as we will also be adding content to the template part.

In order to get to Browse Mode, remember you first need to come out of the editor you might be in, be that the Site or Block Editor. Then, if you have a block theme, under **Appearance**, you can go to **Editor** and enter this mode.

1. Go to **Template Parts**, and after viewing all of the template parts available, you will see an **Add New Template Part** button in the top-right corner. This opens the **Create template part** modal, as shown in the screenshot in *Figure 10.1*:

Figure 10.1 – The interface to create a template part

Once you've clicked to add a template part, you will be able to add a name and select either a **General**, **Header**, or **Footer** area.

2. In our case, let's fill these out to be a header, as shown in the next screenshot:

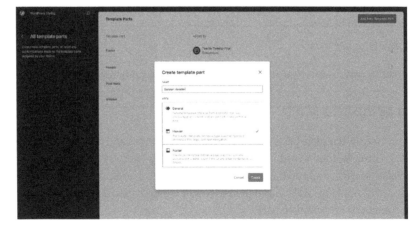

Figure 10.2 – Selecting Header and adding a name

When you click **Create**, this will create a header. The **General** area option is used to create a part that isn't just a header or footer, which are specific template parts. You don't have to create those.

3. Make sure you click **Create**, and then you will be transported to the **Editor** interface, which shows a space to make your template part.

4. Next, we are going to make a header; let's add a **Navigation** block to start. The **Navigation** block is more complicated than other blocks we have looked into before. It is a specific site block and really useful.

As seen in *Figure 10.3*, the **Navigation** block loads up with some default menus if you have any set up – you can find other menus through the **More** menu, which is the three dots lined up. This also has the **Create new menu** option.

Figure 10.3 – Editing the template part

In order to go through this step by step, click **Create new menu** to go through the process of making a new one:

When you select to create a menu, first, you need to select some menu items.

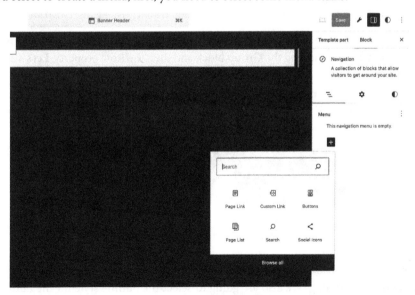

Figure 10.4 – Adding navigation to the template part

These might be page links, custom links, or any other item. We are going to add a page list. This picks up all the pages we have on the site. If you use the + icon, this adds a new menu item, so be sure to fill out each of those details as you go, ensuring you add the link to a page, for example.

Let's add the **Site Logo** block to this header You can add a site logo image by clicking or using drag and drop. Resizing can also be done by using the handles in the side panel. There is a lot to explore here and these blocks are worth taking your time over, one by one.

Now we have a few blocks in this group. Let's select the **Group** block and change to **Row**. To do this, use **List View** to select the **Group** block. Then, in the **Block** styles side panel, select **Transform to Row**. In simple terms, this will align everything on the same row, which is very common for a header. Once we have done this, let's also add some justification to ensure equal spacing. You can see the settings shown in *Figure 10.5*:

Figure 10.5 – Adding a site logo to the template part

As you can see in the preceding figure, once we've done that, everything lines up together. Let's move on to adding a call to action so we can really build up this header beyond just having a logo and navigation.

In *Figure 10.6*, we add a **Cover** block, and then set a header and buttons within – you can use the approach we did previously of adding the **Group** block and then the **Row** property. Let's also add an image to the background of the cover to give maximum visual impact.

Figure 10.6 – Setting a group and row

This creates that **Click to action** header strip that a lot of banners have in their headers. It's a great way of iterating through styling. We also are going to select the outline style for the button and a light coloring.

Before we look at fully creating this template part, you decide whether to show the mobile menu "always" or "just on mobile". For this instance, we are going to show it all the time in this design. Let's see how you set that in the following screenshot, under **Display**:

Figure 10.7 – Setting OVERLAY MENU to Always

There are other settings here for navigation, but for now, let's just set **Always** and leave **ORIENTATION** and **JUSTIFICATION** with their default settings.

Moving on, let's ensure we add the first **Group** block with the logo and the navigation, along with the **Cover** block into that new group. When you do this, as we haven't set any widths it will fit to the smallest size. Let's make sure both groups go full-width of the outer group.

As you can see in *Figure 10.8*, everything is inside **Group**. You can do this by dragging and dropping using **List View**. Now, let's take a look at how we can adjust using the tools designed for padding.

Figure 10.8 – Adding some padding to the group

Remember the **Dimensions** tools? You can see those in the previous screenshot. We will use those to set the padding to the top, bottom, left, and right.

Now that we have our **Header** template part, we can save it. Then, you will see it is available to use. In our next guide, we will see how you can simply replace another template part already existing in a theme.

Replacing a template part

In a later section within this chapter, we're going to explore more ways of interacting with template parts, but a direct method is selecting an existing template part in a theme and then selecting **Replace**:

1. First, switch out the template part in editing mode to the **Blog Home** template so we can begin using the template part we created previously. In the next screenshot, **Header** is selected and you can see the **Replace** option says **Replace Header**. In order to see this, click on the **Header** area first or use **List View** to open the context menu. This will say **Replace** and whatever template part type it is, such as **Replace Header** in our case.

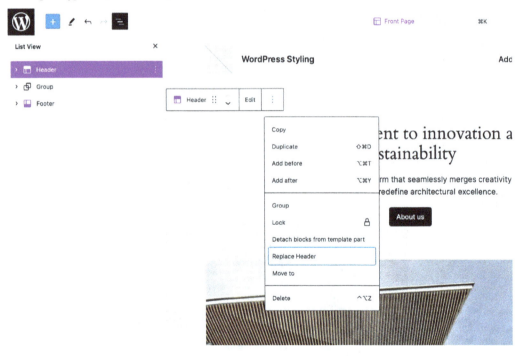

Figure 10.9 – Replacing template part

Let's select to replace it, and you will be taken to a screen where you can view all possible template parts to replace it with.

2. As you can see in *Figure 10.10*, it shows the existing template's template parts.

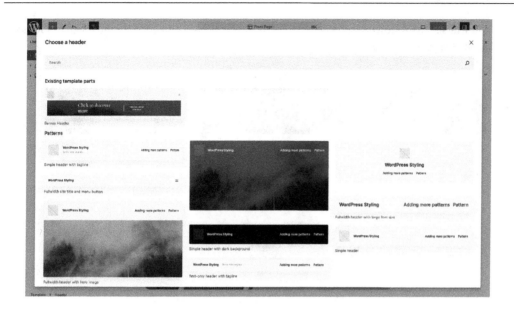

Figure 10.10 – The template part choosing modal

Select the new template part you made. Now you have brought in the new **Header** template part you just created.

3. Once you add a template part, you still have access to all the design tools. For example, in this template part don't forget to add your own site logo.

Figure 10.11 – Adding a site logo

Once that is added, save the new template part and preview it all set in the theme.

4. You will see the following screen, in which it is now the width of the theme itself and looks like it always was designed to fit:

Figure 10.12 – Previewing what we have created

Template parts, as you can see here, are a really powerful way of adding content and creating reusable site elements. The most typical tend to be headers and footers, but as you explore site creation, there are common site elements you will find reused time and time again that fit the idea of template parts. For example, many themes have post meta such as tags and categories or comments as template parts. A lot of default themes also offer them so you can easily learn and discover new approaches.

Using a template part

Template parts are present in most themes and, so far, we've discovered how to create and replace one. What about interacting with them in existing templates?

You can do that by going into each part, and **List View** is a great place to start. Let's see what that looks like in the following screenshot:

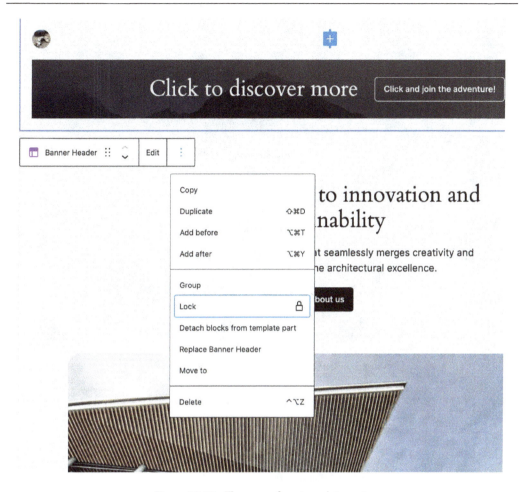

Figure 10.13 – The menu for a template part

In *Figure 10.13*, we can see all the parts of the template part and everything we can do. Let's discover some of those together. The first will be locking.

Exploring locking

This feature is very helpful if you want to prevent the change of a template part. It's worth noting that you can use this feature across anything that contains a block – including patterns and blocks themselves.

In the next screenshot, you can see what happens when you select **Lock** from the menu:

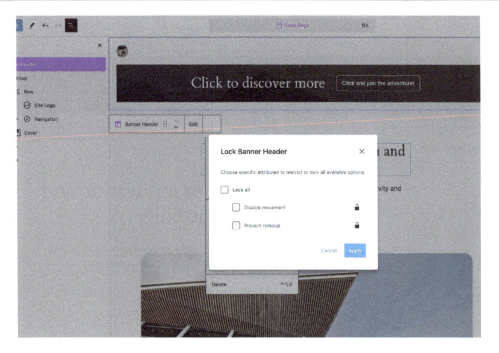

Figure 10.14 – The Lock modal for a template part

Once you have done that, a few options are available for you:

- **Lock all**: This selects everything, which means disabling all movement and preventing removal.
- **Disable movement**: This stops re-ordering or moving without the content itself.
- **Prevent removal**: This prevents deleting the content.

Depending on what you want, check the box and you will see the lock icon apply, and you can click **Apply** to save those settings.

We have discovered locking and learned how incredibly powerful it is. Let's move on with that knowledge into learning how to edit template parts and really level up our knowledge.

Editing a template part

To edit a template part, you simply click **Edit** in the **Block** toolbar. Then, you are taken to the template editing interface where you can use the Site Editor to update the part.

If you want to replace it, you can do that by selecting **Replace**, as you can see in the following screenshot:

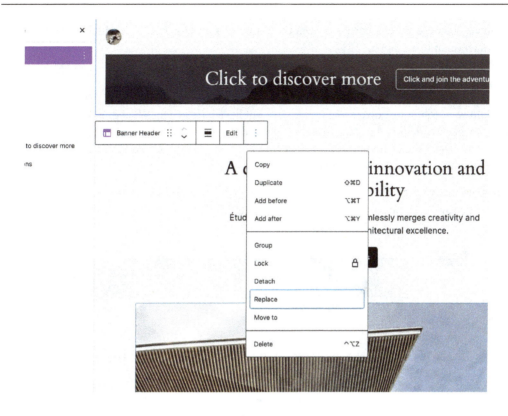

Figure 10.15 – Replacing the template part

Once you click **Replace**, a modal opens allowing you to pick from various options. It's really that easy. Don't forget to save or preview anything you create though.

We now know how to edit a template part, but what about deleting one? There are going to be cases where you might want to not only edit but also completely remove a template part. Let's discover that together now.

Deleting a template part

There are many ways you can remove a template part; let's walk through those together. It's worth noting that the ones listed here are only options that remove them from the template itself, not from the **Template Parts** section of the editor. Only there can it be deleted forever. These are the options:

- Click the **More** (or three-dot) menu and select **Delete**
- Press whatever **Delete** button is within your editor
- Delete in **List View**

You can also manage all template parts from the **Template Parts** interface. We will discover how to do this later on in this chapter.

Detaching a template part

You might want to not just delete a template part, but have it detached. What does this mean? It is similar to where we detached patterns from being synced together. You are saying in this instance just to have it as blocks, the container, and not as a template part. You might want to do this if you want to add something unique just for a single use.

Again, to do this, you can go to the same place on the toolbar and select **Detach** to detach blocks from the template part, as shown in the following screenshot:

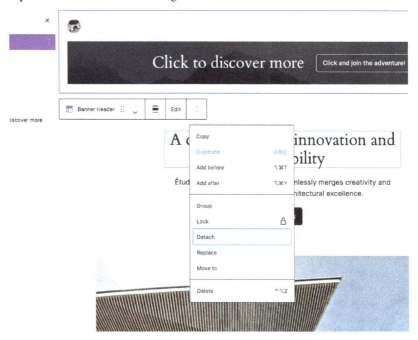

Figure 10.16 – Detaching blocks from the template part

Once you do this, all that happens is the template part for this single case gets detached. Any changes to the original template part will not be reflected in the detached part. You can then go ahead and use the blocks however you want, without impacting every instance of the template part.

Managing a template part

Over time, you likely will gain several template parts. The theme you are using on your site might also have its own template parts. That's where knowing how to manage them comes in useful.

You can see all your template parts under the **Patterns** section within a section that says **Manage all template parts**, as shown in *Figure 10.17*. You can see this in the bottom-left section within the sidebar:

Figure 10.17 – Manage all template parts within the Patterns section

Here, you can see the link to manage, so let's click that and go into them.

Once inside, you get to see all your template parts, as shown in *Figure 10.18*:

Figure 10.18 – A list of all templates and where they are added, showing the one we created

You can see all their details and a list of template parts. It also shows where the template parts came from – for example, the **Twenty Twenty-Four** theme.

Next, you can click on each template part to see more details; for example, a custom template part shows some details about the last revisions with a link.

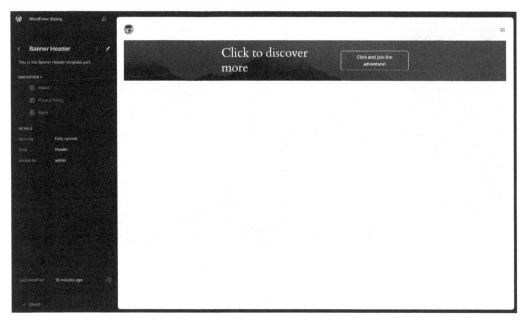

Figure 10.19 – Discovering the details of the template part we created in this chapter

This uses the same interface we saw for patterns, so it should be familiar to you. You can see a summary to the left of everything about this template part. This allows you to see all the details of each part, which you can dive into more, as shown in this next figure:

Figure 10.20 – Editing the template part

From here, you can begin editing and then, once you click **Save**, any changes you make will apply to all template parts that have been made using that one.

As you can see, template parts are powerful, and using them is like we've explored together with blocks and patterns. Once you start using them to create your site content, you can start to really dive into more features of the Site Editor.

Summary

In our journey of discovering the power of the Site Editor, we have begun to explore new features, and this chapter looked at template parts. These go beyond headers and footers to unlock content creation, and many themes come with a range of them already defined.

Let's recap what we did while exploring them together:

- We discovered what template parts are.
- We learned how to use template parts.
- We created a template part together.
- We discovered how to lock template parts.
- We learned how to detach and remove a template part.
- We walked through editing a template part.

With all this knowledge about template parts, we are now going to learn about templates. These are entire layouts, not just parts, and open even more possibilities.

Questions

Answer the following questions to test your understanding of this chapter:

1. What is the definition of a template part?

   a. A part of the site's structure

   b. A header or footer

2. Is this statement true or false? All template parts have to have a Group block to start with.

   a. False

   b. True

3. What does locking do to template parts?

   a. Locks movement, removal, or both of those actions

   b. Locks just movement

   c. Locks just removal

Answers

1. What is the definition of a template part?

    a. A part of the site's structure

2. Is this statement true or false? All template parts have to have a Group block to start with.

    b. False

3. What does locking do to template parts?

    a. Locks movement, removal, or both of those actions

Reference

Learn more about templates and template parts from the developer handbook:

```
https://developer.wordpress.org/themes/block-themes/templates-and-
template-parts/#block-c5fa39a2-a27d-4bd2-98d0-dc6249a0801a
```

11
Discovering and Creating Templates

In the previous chapter, we discovered template parts – self-contained sections of blocks that you can put into site content. In this chapter, we are going to discover templates themselves.

When the term *template* is used, it often refers to the entire layout of a section of a site – for example, the page or post seen. It might be for a page, a post, or a particular type of content. You can even get specific templates for a particular post or plugin. There is an almost never-ending possibility of variations. You can create your own template, but most themes also come with them.

In this chapter, we will discover the following together:

- Managing templates
- Creating a template
- Using a template
- Editing a template
- Deleting a template

We will then wrap up what we have learned about templates and move on to close our exploration of templates by looking at setting a front page and how we can be inspired. Our journey into discovering content continues.

Managing templates

One of the first things you will want to do with templates is explore and manage them. You can handle these tasks through a very similar interface to that for patterns and template parts. Let's go through the process together here:

1.   Click **Templates** in the Site Editor, as shown in *Figure 11.1*.

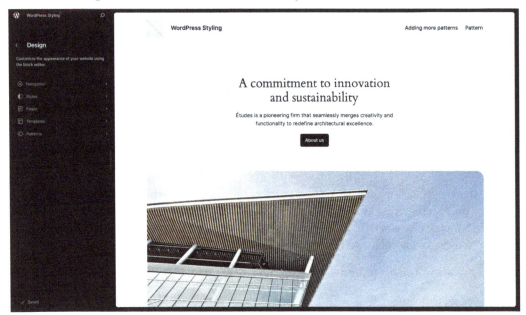

Figure 11.1 – Templates showing in the side panel of the Site Editor

This is the view we've been using for a few chapters now as we discover and explore the Site Editor together.

On clicking the **Templates** link, you are shown all the templates used by the currently activated theme. We're using the Twenty Twenty-Four default WordPress theme. As you can see in *Figure 11.2*, there are a range of templates it comes with.

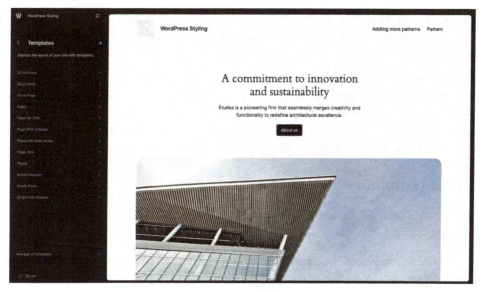

Figure 11.2 – The Templates interface

As you can see, there are many things you can do from this section. You can click on each template, create a new one, and even search for others.

2. Let's click on **Blog Home** to discover more about this template as the following screenshot shows. We explored this template earlier in *Chapter 9*.

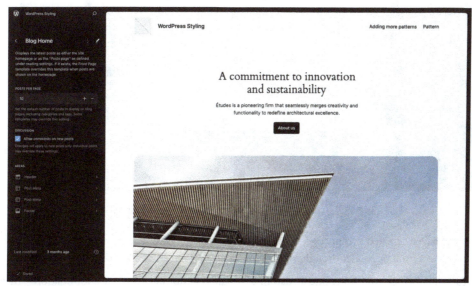

Figure 11.3 – A summary of a template

The side panel shows us many more details about the template, with the template itself being displayed to the right. This offers a great overview of the template. You can also interact with and adjust anything you might want here.

Managing templates is straightforward and uses an interface we've already become familiar with. As we begin to go further into creating templates, we will also be using some interfaces we have explored already. One of the foundations of site editing is to use the same interface for similar actions. The way this works is by using the same interface while interacting with patterns, template parts, and templates. This helps you learn to do something once and apply it to other actions – it opens more possibilities.

Creating a template

Whilst managing is great, being able to create your own is even better. Let's together start to learn how to add a template:

1. From the **Templates** section click the + icon, next to **Templates** in the left sidebar. This is how you add a template. As shown in *Figure 11.4*, a modal will open giving you options for the type of template you want to create.

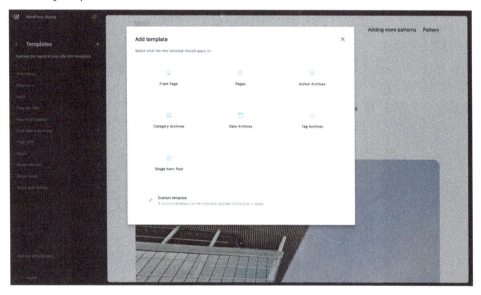

Figure 11.4 – Adding a template and being given options

If you haven't created a front page, then this would be also shown here as an option. We are going to create a front page later though, so for now let's look at creating a template for a specific page.

You will also see you can create a custom template that doesn't even use a foundation – there really are so many options you can choose from.

2. Select **Page** and you will see the following modal open.

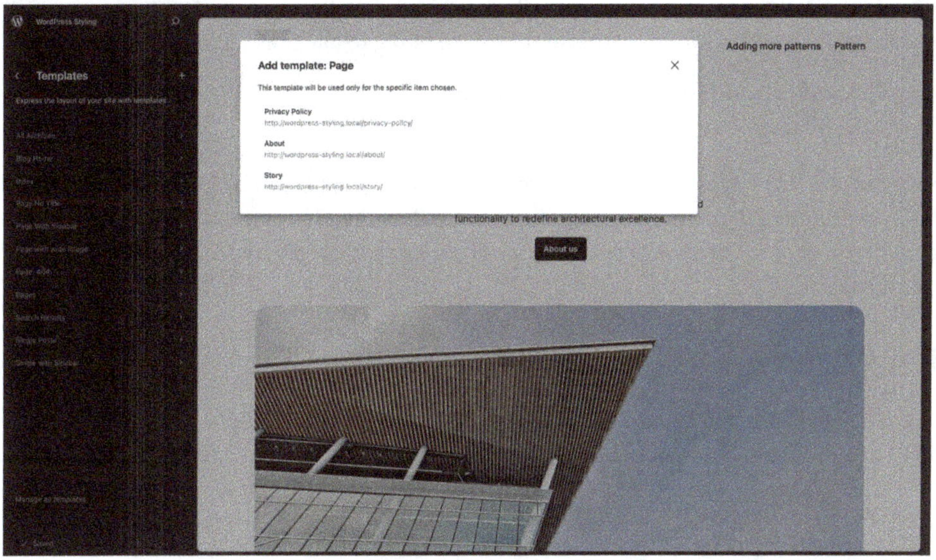

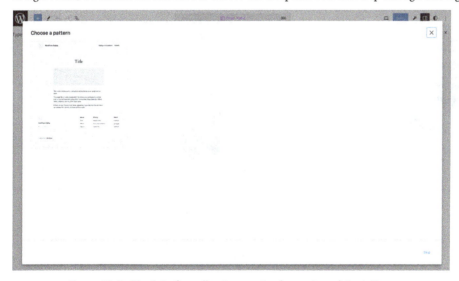

Figure 11.5 – Creating a page template for the Sample page

The modal shows a list of all the pages you can create templates for. In our site example, we can create for a few pages; let's select **About**. You simply select that page and you will then be taken to a modal allowing you to select a template design.

3. In *Figure 11.6*, we can see the interface to choose our template. Let's now step through that together.

Figure 11.6 – The interface allowing you to choose template options

You can always change this in any way you want. You also can start with a blank template should you want – it's up to you; after all, it's your site. If you want to select this pattern, click it; otherwise, select **Skip**. In our example, we are going to click the pattern.

4. Once we have clicked the pattern, the Site Editor will load with that pattern applied to your template. It's as easy as that to set a template to whatever you want.

Creating templates this way is a great method of customizing your site to be just how you want. You can adapt your content depending on what it is and reflect the differences across your site. From having a different-looking archive depending on the category to employing a unique 404 page – the choice is yours!

Editing a template

Now we are familiar with how to create and manage templates. Let's next explore how to take existing templates and edit them. You will notice we are going to use the familiar interface again. Let's step right in:

1. Click through from the **Templates** section and pick **Blog Home** again. You will see the template summary view as shown in the following screenshot.

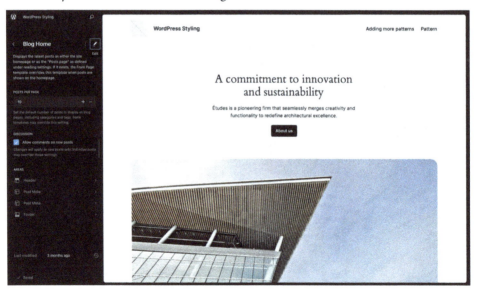

Figure 11.7 – The template summary for Blog Home

From here, you can click the template itself, or the *pen* icon next to the **Blog Home** title (or the respective name of the template you are viewing), to edit it. Let's do that now and the Site Editor will open.

2. Once that is open, you can edit this template. Notice that **Blog Home** is showing at the top? That indicates we're on that template.

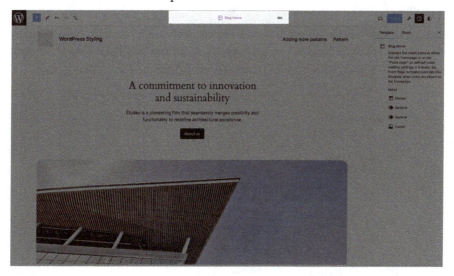

Figure 11.8 – Editing Blog Home

Now we have this interface open, we can make any changes we want and then click **Save** to have our changes reflected across any content on our site that uses this template.

3. Let's now change that template to make it unique for our site. First, we are going to add a background and some padding around a section. You can see that in *Figure 11.9*.

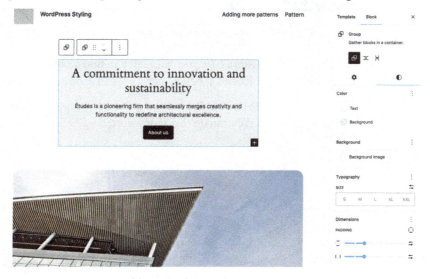

Figure 11.9 – Adding a background color and some padding

Once we've done that, we can select by clicking the **Command Palette**, which then offers you some options. That's in the top-center of the editor as shown in the preceding figure; it says **Blog Home**.

4. Click **Blog Home**. As you can see in the next screenshot, when you click this, you get a menu to search the **Command Palette**. Let's get a few more options by selecting the group block and pressing *Cmd + K* (Mac) or *Ctrl + K* (Windows) or clicking the **Blog Home** section.

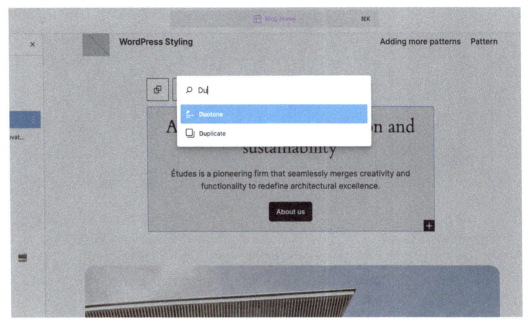

Figure 11.10 – Command Palette options

Once we have this selected as in *Figure 11.10*, you can search to find a range of options. This is a great shortcut for tasks we have looked at before, but it's worth showing it in context here.

5. If you click the WordPress logo (the stylized **W**) in the top-left corner, you are taken back to the summary of the template again. You can do this at any time.

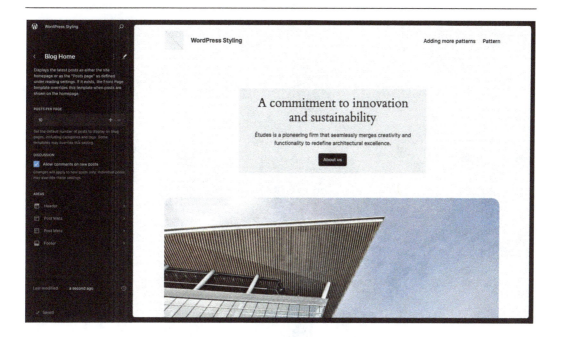

Figure 11.11 – Showing the template summary

Templates like this **Blog Home** one are really powerful. You have seen how, with just these simple adjustments, you can truly make your own template quite quickly for any section on your site.

Using a template

Most of the templates work automatically due to something called the **template hierarchy** that we will explore later together in the next chapter.

If you go to the editor, you can see in the right panel an area named **Template**. You can also apply templates from here should you wish. This is a way to override or apply specific templates.

Let's look at how this can be applied in the Block Editor as this method was typical for templates before the Site Editor existed. Within the Site Editor, you do not get the dropdown to apply a template as you do within the Block Editor. You can see in the next screenshot how applying a template works in the Block Editor with your content.

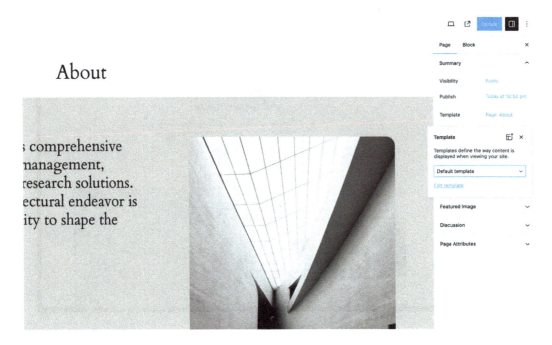

Figure 11.12 – Applying a template to a page

Once you select a template from the **Template** drop-down, the new template will be applied. It's a really easy method, but don't forget to click **Update** and also preview the page.

Deleting a template

Now that you have your templates applied, there might come a point where you need to delete at least one. It's easy to do this via the same interface we have been using throughout our work with templates. As shown in the following screenshot, at the top left, next to the editing icon, there is a three-vertical-dots button. Click this, it is also called "more menu" and you will see the **Delete** option. This only applies to templates created on the site and not to templates provided by the theme, which can't be deleted using this interface. Deleting theme templates on one site isn't recommended if you want to use updating in the future.

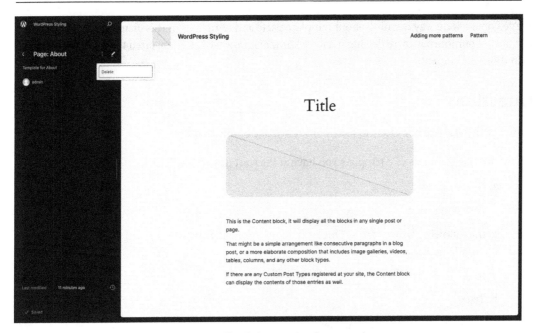

Figure 11.13 – The Delete option for a template

Templates are powerful, but sometimes you want to start fresh. You can do this by deleting it from the template overview under **Manage all templates**.

There is so much we've discovered in this chapter. Let's now finish up by summarizing what we've learned together.

Summary

In our journey of discovering the power of the Site Editor, we have begun to explore new features. We have learned what templates are and have now leveled up our understanding of the sites we create and how they come together. Along the way, we learned how site blocks add to our content.

Let's recap what we have learned in this chapter:

- We discovered what templates are.
- We created a template together.
- We understood how to apply a template.
- We learned how to manage, edit, and delete templates.

We've come a long way learning about template parts and templates in this chapter. Let's close out this part of our journey by reviewing what we know and how we can be inspired to create even more incredible site content.

Questions

Answer the following questions to test your knowledge of this chapter:

1. What is the name of a template you have at the start of your site?

    a. A front page

    b. A starting page

2. Is the following true or false? One of the foundations of site editing is to reuse the interface for similar actions.

    a. False

    b. True

3. Do all themes come with templates?

    a. No, templates are always optional and many don't include them.

    b. Yes, because even an index file is a template.

Answers

1. What is the name of a template you have at the start of your site?

    a. A front page

2. Is the following true or false? One of the foundations of site editing is to reuse the interface for similar actions.

    b. True

3. Do all themes come with templates?

    b. Yes, because even an index file is a template.

12

Templates Wrap-Up

We have been on quite a journey with templates. We have looked at the Site Editor and reviewed template parts and templates – our journey has been extensive through the interface and hierarchy.

In this chapter, we will discover the following together:

- The possibilities of templates
- Setting a front page
- Getting inspiration

Once we have done this, let's finish with a summary and review what we have learned. Then we are going to move on to looking at themes themselves as we complete our journey together.

The possibilities of templates

Themes are great, but you can extend their potential using templates and go beyond their initial offering. You can achieve more with just one theme by changing a pattern or template. Templates provide a way for you to style specific content, such as a post, a category, or even a front page.

The following are a few examples of when templates are useful:

- **To style specific posts from a category or a tag**: Think of having a "Dogs" category and being able to style all content under that tag with a specific template.
- **To style content published on a specific date, such as a holiday or event**: Perhaps you have a date archive for a holiday to an island retreat and have a template just for that.
- **To apply different templates to posts by specific authors:** You could, for example, add different author bios and specific information for each author in each template.

There is a lot more, but these examples give you a taste of what you can do with templates.

Many themes come with a set of predefined templates that you can apply or customize using the methods we've already walked through. It really is as simple as that to create a range of custom options using the editor.

Template hierarchy

Most of using a template just happens. However, this is due to something in WordPress called the **template hierarchy**.

The template hierarchy is a foundational principle of WordPress, describing the order of preference in which WordPress applies templates. For example, if the front-page template doesn't exist, it looks for the next template further up the hierarchy. You can override this hierarchy by creating specific templates.

> **Note**
> The template hierarchy can get quite complex. If you want to learn more about it, you can do so here: `https://developer.wordpress.org/themes/basics/template-hierarchy/`

Now we've learned a bit more about templates, their possibilities, and the template hierarchy. Let's move on to creating a very common template ourselves – that of the front page.

Setting a front page

Many themes have a front page by default. So, you can always pick that template and activate it, or you can create your own. Let's walk through creating one using the interface in the editor.

1. Click to Add template using the + icon next to **Templates**. See *Figure 12.1*.

Figure 12.1: Modal to add a template

As you can see, you are given the option right away to add a **Front Page** template as that hasn't been set up yet. Let's click that option.

2. You will notice you are given some predefined templates as options. These come with your given theme, and some will work due to the template hierarchy falling back to using the next template. See *Figure 12.2*.

Figure 12.2: The Choose a pattern modal

You can of course create your own templates or patterns, but let's select one of these. To do that, click on your chosen option. Once you do, it will load up and you can begin to use it.

Now you have a front page you can start to use. Don't forget to save it!

We have a basic understanding now of the template hierarchy and templates. Let's move on to adding the power of site blocks to those templates, starting with the **Query Loop** block.

Query Loop block

This block is often at the heart of most of your template's work. It is literally what shows the content. You will often hear this referred to as the **Query Loop** because it loops through your content depending on the settings and gets a set number of posts.

This block should be added to specific templates, such as the front page and archive templates to ensure they output the content on the frontend of your site. Being aware of which templates need these functional blocks is helpful and the Site Editor has warning messages to guide you.

You also can look at existing themes such as Twenty Twenty-Four for guidance when creating your own templates. Be careful when deleting anything and always preview your template before going live.

In this example, we are going to use a template without a pattern to see what that looks like. To do this, you go through the same process of adding a template but don't select at the modal stage. We then are going to add a **Query Loop** block.

The first stage of the **Query Loop** block starts by asking you to **Choose** a pattern or **Start blank** without a template. Let's walk through together how to use this block.

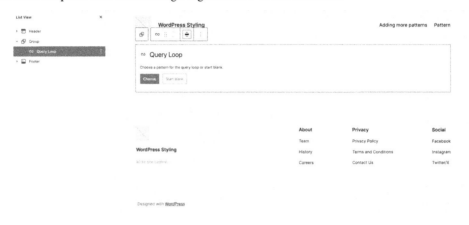

Figure 12.3: Query Loop in the Site Editor

If you select **Choose**, you will then be presented with a range of patterns to select from. You can see that in *Figure 12.4*.

Figure 12.4: Choosing a Query Loop pattern

These patterns all output the same content; it's the visual layout that differs. Some come from the theme and some from the block itself.

To select one, simply click it and it will be used.

After you select a pattern, the editor will refresh, and the pattern will be loaded.

In the following screenshot, you can see the **Query Loop** block with the chosen pattern and the settings open in the panel.

Figure 12.5: The Query Loop block in the Site Editor with the settings open

Once the **Query Loop** block appears in the editor, you can adjust anything else you want in the side panel. In this example, under **List View**, you can see the contents of **Query Loop**. The **Post Template** block contains the pattern you selected.

Pagination

Let's look at an important block here – **Pagination**. This has a lot of different display settings as you can see in the side panel, including justification and alignment options – you can even set arrows or chevrons as styles to the pagination navigation elements.

Figure 12.6: Pagination block with settings open

Pagination is just one specific block that is important to the **Query Loop** block. You can see in our example other things including a **Post Template** and even a template part for **Post Meta**, which is within the **Post Template** block – not visible in the screenshot in *Figure 12.6*. Not every pattern will use all these parts; for example, it might not always have a template part for **Post Meta**. Each theme and pattern will handle things differently.

Having a template for **Post Meta** is quite common as a use case for template parts. We all too often think of template parts as just referring to headers and footers, but it's not true. Having access to repeated parts of content, such as **Post Meta** (the publication date and information about a post), is useful.

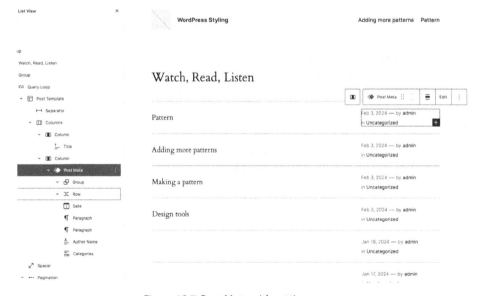

Figure 12.7: Post Meta with settings open

In the preceding screenshot, you can see how it's closed off at the editor level because it's a template part. You must click **Edit** to interact when the **Template part** block is selected. Once you select one of the blocks from **List View**, you can edit it directly from the template interface, without needing to switch to the template part interface. This is one key benefit of using template parts: you are literally separating the site by going into each part as you edit.

In this next screen, you can see this happening: the **Edit** link has been clicked and the template part has been loaded in the editor.

Figure 12.8: Post Meta template part view

In this way, your focus is kept on the task at hand. It's easy to get things done when you have the tools and interface options you need, and none of the things you don't.

We have learned a lot about some specific blocks so far, and have gone further into blocks such as the **Query Loop**. Now let's move on to how we can get inspired and apply our knowledge to our creations.

Getting inspiration

Previously, we explored inspiration for patterns. If you are looking for inspiration or templates, the sources are similar. Carefully examine some sites online that you find interesting. Start to break them down into sections and consider what elements are used to build them. For example, which parts could be repeat sections via template parts or patterns? How would they be formed?

It might be useful to start a digital scrapbook or just to start sketching in block format, a practice often referred to as *napkin sketches*. Another tip to consider is to think of the user experience. While having lots of templates and variations might seem great, what is it going to be like for the end user? What do you like encountering on other sites and what works in your target market?

A key to success is to look at other examples of similar sites to the one you are creating. Be inspired by those who have created before you. Start small and iterate once you know what works for you. Don't start with hundreds of templates and then scale back.

You can also try on different themes for size, testing out their front pages and various templates – see what they are like and get inspiration from there. The default themes for WordPress are a great place to start, as they are free to use.

It's worth noting, as we wrap up our journey through templates, that many specific plugins and sites have different templates for certain functional aspects – for example, a checkout page on a WooCommerce shop, or a basket to see everything you have chosen to purchase so far. Perhaps a list of all membership activity on a membership site. Often, templates can come with a plugin or a companion theme that works with the plugin.

This ends our journey together through templates. We've learned a lot. So, let's now summarize everything.

Summary

Templates have a lot of possibilities. In this chapter, we explored some of these, looking at how to create custom ones and considering what they could be used for.

Let's recap what we now can do after our exploration:

- We learned the types of templates and what they could be used for.
- We learned about the template hierarchy and what it means.
- We discovered how to set a front-page template.
- We learned about new site blocks such as the Query Loop block.
- We discovered that template parts don't just mean headers and footers, they also can include site meta.
- We looked at where to go for inspiration.

Templates and template parts are powerful, but they come together in a theme. In our next chapter, together, let's look at what themes are, the history of themes, and how themes have changed. We are going to take our knowledge of the Site Editor even further by exploring global styles, and then put it all together to conclude this rapid journey through all things styling in WordPress.

Questions

Answer the following questions to test your knowledge of this chapter:

1. Template parts can only be used for site headers or footers. True or false?

   a. True

   b. False

2. If you wanted to set a page for a site to start on, what would you select when adding a template?

    a. Front page

    b. Starting page

    c. Main page

3. A template that lists posts is called which of the following?

    a. A post list

    b. An archive

4. The block that outputs posts is called which of the following?

    a. The Loop block

    b. The Loop Query block

    c. The Query Loop block

Answers

1. Template parts can only be used for site headers or footers. True or false?

    b. False

2. If you wanted to set a page for a site to start on, what would you select when adding a template?

    a. Front page

3. A template that lists posts is called which of the following?

    b. An archive

4. The block that outputs posts is called which of the following?

    c. The Query Loop block

Part 4:
Themes

WordPress themes have changed. In *Part 4*, you will explore styles and block themes to unlock the power of the Site Editor and blocks.

This section has the following chapters:

13

Understanding How Themes Have Changed

Until now, we have looked only at *parts* of themes. We've not really examined themes themselves in their entire form. We are going to move past that now and start considering themes as an entire package.

In this chapter, we will discover the following together:

- A brief history of themes
- The changing nature of themes
- The new possibilities – no more code

After this background around themes and learning how they have changed, we will take that knowledge into the next chapter where we will learn about site styles.

A brief history of themes

Themes in many respects have been an essential part of the success of WordPress. From the first default theme through to the new concept of block themes and the latest default theme as of writing this book, themes have been at the heart and literal front of WordPress sites.

They are seen by and are familiar to many, even if they don't work with WordPress. Take Kubrick for example, as shown in the following screenshot. This was the default theme for WordPress 1.5 to 2.9.

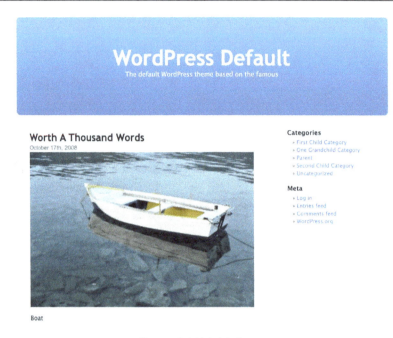

Figure 13.1: Kubrick theme

Lots of people would recognize the look of this theme even if they were unaware of its name or that it is from WordPress. Many of those who create WordPress themes also learned by examining the code of Kubrick and other similar themes due to themes being open source.

Now we've laid the foundation of what themes were, let's look at what a theme is today and the types of themes available.

What is a theme?

A loose definition of a theme is a set of template files and a style that defines a site's appearance. Think of it as a package that, once activated, allows you to have every element of your site look a particular way – that is, themed the same.

Themes can be found and activated using the theme directory within WordPress, or you can use the WordPress.org theme directory: https://wordpress.org/themes/. We will look a little later at how you can discover more themes on your own.

Commercial themes

There are many terms you will hear around themes; one of those is **commercial themes**; you might also hear **premium themes** used. This typically means a theme you pay for. The theme could be a site builder, a framework, or a theme that works for a specific plugin or a particular type of site, such as a shop.

These themes can be bought from sellers themselves; they can also be brought from theme marketplaces.

Often it can be hard to tell what is a framework and what is a theme – the terms get confusing. For example, many themes could get labelled a framework which is literally a foundation to build from. This isn't something we're going to explore in this book but is worth saying here. With the Site Editor and the changes made to themes, some simplification has happened, and this is what we will explore now.

Theme check

The Themes team is a group of volunteer contributors within WordPress who manage the theme directory. This team has established a series of requirements and a checking process for themes.

These are the standards that all themes must pass to be accepted and vary depending on the type of theme. Think of this as quality control for themes. All themes within the WordPress theme directory have gone through this process.

Now let's move on and see how themes have changed. We have looked at the history of themes and what a theme is, but what have they become today?

The changing nature of themes

Many changes have occurred, not only in the process of creating a theme but also in terms of how you add content and even styling. This also brings a change in the terminology used. You will for example come across two main terms when exploring themes: **Classic** and **Block** themes. Let's go through both of those terms now, learn what they mean, and discover the differences between them.

> **Note**
>
> In this book, we aren't going to spend an extensive amount of time creating a theme together, as we are going to be exploring many other aspects related to styling. There are many resources to dive further into this topic if you wish, one of which is `https://developer.wordpress.org/themes`.

Over the years, themes have changed, but it is worth considering why this was needed in the first place. Here are just a few reasons:

- Switching between themes meant often a total rework of content and the loss of formatting.
- You could end up being tied to a framework ecosystem along with WordPress to get even basic site-editing functionality.
- The user experience of options and other settings was totally different between themes. This meant that, for example, the same setting would be in a different place from theme to theme.
- Most simple customizations required the end user to understand CSS and even more complex coding.

Simply put, themes required advanced skills just to do simple things.

Now we know why themes needed to change. Let's look at the types of themes we have now. You might come across the term hybrid used for themes that use just a `block.json`. To keep it simple we will refer to two types.

Classic themes

This is what most people think of as a theme. It typically uses a language called PHP for its parts and content. It will, within the files, use code called a `loop` to display the content of a site.

Often a classic theme has widget areas, sidebars, and uses the **Customizer** to let users set custom colors, typography, and other features.

Block themes

Block themes are increasingly becoming the standard for themes, and we've looked at them throughout this book so far without giving a name to them. They use HTML files and contain blocks in those files. They also might use CSS and JS, just like classic themes, but they don't have to as you can use `theme.json`, native components, and design tools.

In many respects, the advances brought by block themes resolved the issues of classic themes as you can now change them without losing your settings. They use the same interface to do the styling and the styles are applied through design tools.

Different but the same

Often the two types of themes can seem different, as illustrated here, but they also share common features. They both use the template hierarchy, which we discovered in *Chapter 12*.

We will briefly now understand a little more as to why the differences are important and how the changes empower us.

The new possibilities – no more code

While themes in the past typically required you to be either the end-user or a theme developer to use them, new tools such as design tools and the Site Editor have opened a lot more possibilities to everyone, no matter whether they can code or not.

This is one major empowerment of the way the new block themes work: not only by providing powerful design tools and styling opportunities but by standardizing the interface for things that previously required code. From typography to complex layouts and opacity, background positioning, and even sticky positions – block themes come alive through the editing experience by using tools.

Themes can have tools set on or off within them. Perhaps you don't want to allow specific ones, that is possible using the theme file settings. There are also system defaults built into WordPress, for example, default palette colors, typography, and more.

By removing the need to know so much code, more people can create the vision they have in their minds. This means that people no longer need to resort to grabbing code from the internet, which in most cases they might not understand too well

This in turn helps improve the quality of the web itself.

Summary

In this chapter, we have taken a first look at themes in their entirety, considering what a theme is and how they have changed over the history of WordPress.

Let's recap what we have explored together:

- We now know what a theme is.
- We discovered how themes have changed and why they needed to change.
- We learned what classic and block themes are.
- We discovered the new possibilities provided by themes.

Now that we have this information, let's move on to an important aspect of themes, global styles. Global styles combined with design tools unlock the styling for block themes – so let's understand together what global styles are and how they work.

Questions

Answer the following questions to test your knowledge of this chapter:

1. Which of the following is the definition of a theme?

    a. A theme is a set of template files and a style that defines a site's appearance.

    b. A collection of templates, parts, and CSS stylesheets along with JavaScript files, which must include the original source files.

2. Which of the following is not a type of theme?

    a. Block themes

    b. Classic themes

    c. Fixed themes

3. A theme that must be paid for is called what?

    a. A commercial theme

    b. A freemium theme

    c. A pricey theme

Answers

1. Which of the following is the definition of a theme?

   a. A theme is a set of template files and a style that defines a site's appearance.

2. Which of the following is not a type of theme?

   c. Fixed themes

3. A theme that must be paid for is called what?

   a. A commercial theme

14
Discovering Styles

The previous chapter looked at the history of themes. We discovered why themes needed to change and how they have changed. We began to learn about classic and block themes, discovering new terminology along the way.

Now, we are going to move along with unlocking the power of styling through a concept known as **Global Styles**. It's worth noting that during the time of writing this book, the interface and concept was changed to **Styles** rather than Global Styles. We will from this point refer to Global Styles as Styles; however, a lot of documentation will refer to it as Global Styles.

In this chapter, we will discover the following together:

- What are Styles?
- A walkthrough of the Styles interface
- Style variations
- Discovering the Style Book

Styles within the Site Editor unlock powerful interfaces where, previously, you would have had to know either CSS or a particular interface. Let's now discover together what they are and how to use them.

What are Styles?

In simple terms, Styles, set styling across the entire site. They can be accessed from the Site Editor but impact the entire range of your content. Within the Site Editor, there is a section under the Styles icon that contains a number of sections:

- **Typography**: You can manage the typography settings, from text to links and much more.
- **Colors**: Here, you will find custom and global palettes and even gradients.
- **Layout**: This allows you to control the structure of your entire site.
- **Blocks**: You can adjust each block-specific setting.

We are going to be exploring this interface in more depth together later in this chapter. This is just an overview of what Styles are. Now, let's move on and discover why we need Styles.

Why do we need Styles?

The first question probably should be what do Styles solve and why do they exist?

One of the big issues with themes we talked about previously was having to know complex code to do simple things. What Styles do is empower anyone to make styling changes with a consistent interface. In the past, you had to learn the interface of each theme – it might have changed from theme to theme. There is now a consistent set of tools within WordPress itself.

A walkthrough of the Styles interface

In order to discover Styles, let's first walk through this together; after all, learning by doing is powerful.

We are going to use the default theme, Twenty Twenty-Four, as our base to explore Styles. First, let's go to **Appearance** and click **Site Editor**. See *Figure 14.1*.

Figure 14.1 – Styles in the editor menu

Here, you can see the **Styles** menu. What you see in *Figure 14.1* might vary depending on your theme and content; however, the left interface will remain consistent. Let's click the menu option for **Styles**.

Once you select it, you are presented with, as shown in *Figure 14.2*, an opportunity to pick a Style.

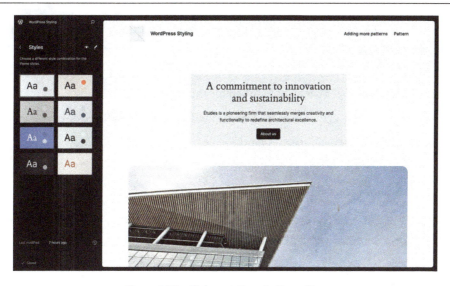

Figure 14.2 – Style variations in the editor

The default Twenty Twenty-Four theme has multiple Styles, as you can see in *Figure 14.2*, and we will explore what that means later. For now, click the pencil icon, next to the **Styles** heading, and we can go into the interface to work with this Style. This is known as the Style variation overview.

In this example, it is important to note that we are adding a custom Style in addition, not overwriting the existing one. We aren't changing the theme or causing anything that edits the core files.

In *Figure 14.3*, we can see the Site Editor's Style interface.

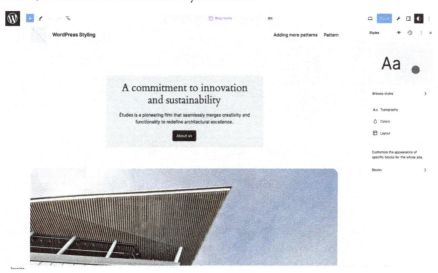

Figure 14.3 – Styles in the Site Editor

Figure 14.3 shows, by default, a summary tile of the style. This is the same as it shows when you view all styles as shown in *Figure 14.2*, the Style variation overview. From this section, you can interact with Styles and then do various things:

- **Browse styles**: See other Styles within the editor and try them out.

- **Typography**: This shows the Styles for typography, for example headings, links or text.

- **Colors**: This shows the color palettes for the Style.

- **Layout**: This shows the settings for layout.

- **Blocks**: This allows you to create styles per block.

Let's now take the default style and change the link color. To do that, go to Colors and select Link to open the palette, as shown in *Figure 14.4*:

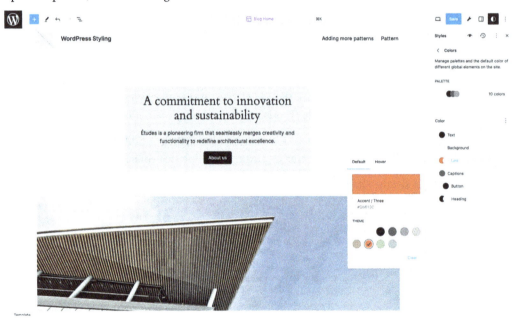

Figure 14.4 – Adding a custom Link style

As shown in *Figure 14.4*, you will see a palette has already been loaded to pick from – this is declared by the theme and is something you can choose from.

It's worth mentioning here the difference between default palettes and custom ones. Most themes will come with pre-defined palettes. However, you can create your own custom palettes. To do that, you simply click **Palette** and the manager for custom palettes opens, as shown in *Figure 14.5*:

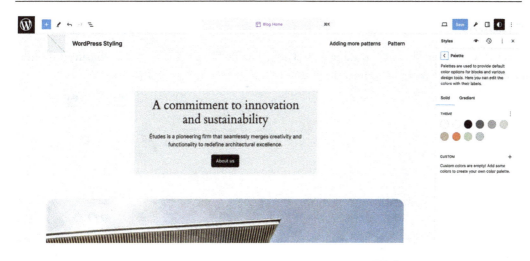

Figure 14.5 – Custom palette interface

Here, you can add your own custom colors, which will be available for anyone to pick.

We adjusted the link color. So, let's click **Save**, and you will see the following screen telling you there are **Custom Styles**. See *Figure 14.6*.

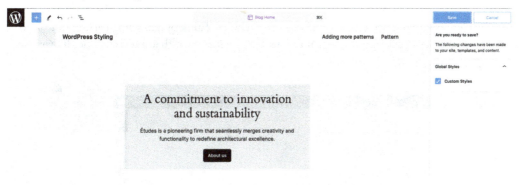

Figure 14.6 – Saving Custom Styles

This message shown in the screenshot saying what has changed is very helpful. You have created your own custom Style. Click **Save**, and you now have a custom style for your site.

As you can see, changing something across your entire site is incredibly easy – but you can also make complex adjustments from the same interface at the block or layout level.

Now, we are going to move on to look at other functions within this styling interface. There are a few icons we haven't reviewed. So, let's go back and look at them.

Revisions

It can easily get complex when working with styling like this. There is, however, a built-in revisions functionality that you can find under the clock-like icon shown in *Figure 14.7*.

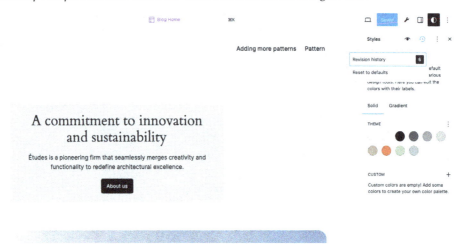

Figure 14.7 – Revisions menu options

Here, you can reset to the defaults, which is self-explanatory. Think of it as going back in time. This is where you can step back one revision at a time. Let's look at what that interface looks like in the following screenshot:

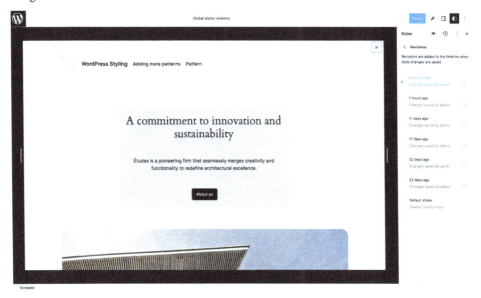

Figure 14.8 – Revision steps

As you can see in *Figure 14.8,* you can see each change you have made and step through them. To go back to each step, you simply click, and it will show them. This is a great way of finding out where you might have made a change, what happened, and even reverting to it.

Revisions are incredibly helpful as you layer more styling onto your content. Knowing how to see where changes occurred allows you the confidence to make changes because you can just step into the interface and easily go back to a previous revision.

Adjusting block by block

We've shown so far how you can adjust based on the entire site, but what about a specific block throughout the site? You can do that by clicking **Blocks** and finding the one you want. Let's do that now by selecting **Quote**.

In the next screenshot, you can see the blocks set out, which allows you to go into each block to view the styling:

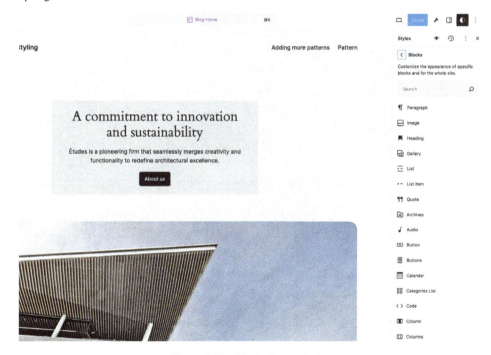

Figure 14.9 – Block view in Styles

From this screen shown in *Figure 14.9,* you can pick any block and apply a style. Let's select the **Quote** block and move on to *Figure 14.10* to apply a style.

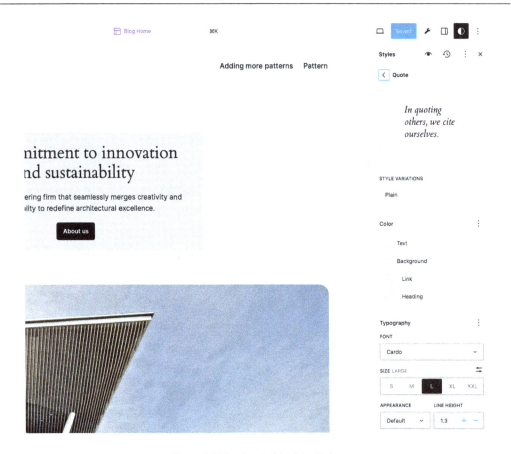

Figure 14.10 – Quote block in Styles

Here, we can see the interface for the styling options for the **Quote** block. You have a summary tile, just like for the Style itself. This is helpful for seeing what the style is by default. Then you have all the options you can adjust.

Let's add a background color and change the text color. To do that, click on the circle to add a color from the theme palettes or a new custom color.

In the following screenshot, we can see what the **Quote** block looks like when we start to add some styling:

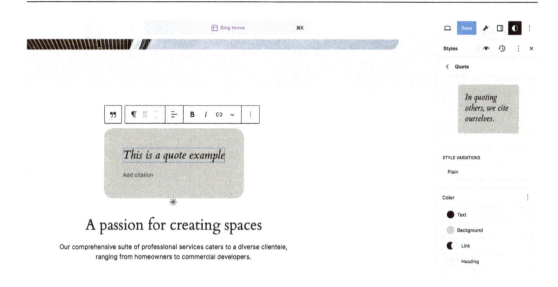

Figure 14.11 – Custom style for quote blocks

Remember to save the style you have been working on, and you now have quotes styled throughout your site just how you want.

As you can see, it's simple to create a style, but sometimes you might want to go a little further. We've not discovered a function many want, which is custom CSS – let's do that together now.

Additional CSS

While one of the goals of Styles is to not have to add custom CSS, you can still bring your own custom CSS in if you want to.

You can find custom CSS under the dotted menu (this is often referred to as a kebab menu within interface design due to how it looks). Once you're there, select **Additional CSS,** and the interface opens.

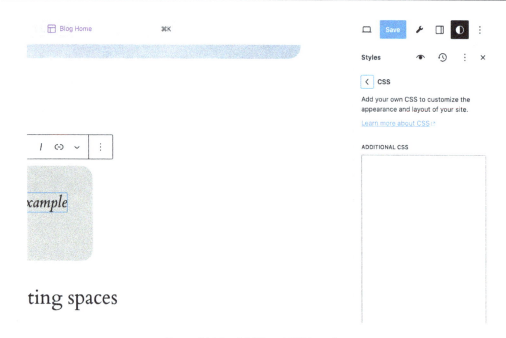

Figure 14.12 – Additional CSS interface

You can add any CSS you want here, and it will be saved and used within your site. There is the option to add custom CSS to each block within the editor. This is not something you are typically going to need until you get deeper into your styling adventures. Knowing where these interfaces are right now is the most important information.

We've discovered a lot in our journey through styling, and there is one powerful feature we haven't explored yet: multiple styles within one theme. Let's do that now.

Style variations

In the past, a concept known as child themes was often used for simple styling variations of themes. Now, there is the option to have multiple styles in one theme using something called `theme.json` and having a base file, with others within a folder.

> **Note**
>
> The `theme.json` file is not something we are going to dive deeply into within this book, as we aren't exploring code. However, you can learn a lot more at `https://developer.wordpress.org/themes/global-settings-and-styles/`. In simple terms, it's a recipe file that has all the settings for the theme.

Let's take a look at how a default theme, for example, Twenty Twenty-Four, uses style variations.

As we discovered before, when we opened the Site Editor, the default Style was selected. Let's now click Onyx to see what that does.

Figure 14.13 – Style variations showing in Editor

As you should see, it changes the view to that theme. You can select different styles this way you can try styling on before you click Save and activate on your site.

Changing your styling like this was previously a lot more work to create within the theme and change from the interface. Styles open an easy switch with these simple clicks. There is also the ability to see the impact of a Style on the blocks across a site. Let's now explore Style Book together.

Discovering the Style Book

It is great we can create our own Styles and vary the default styles; however, sometimes you want to see how each block and element is impacted. There is something called Style Book built into the Site Editor.

From inside the Styles interface in the Site Editor, select the eye icon and you will see the following interface open:

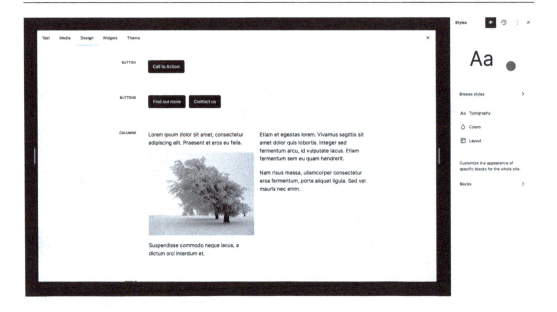

Figure 14.14– Style Book in the Site Editor

This is the Style Book, and it shows each block with the Style applied. This is incredibly helpful for seeing both what is impacted and what changes you might want to make to create the perfect styling for you.

One thing you can also do within this interface is grab the sidebars and drag in the view. This then provides a change in screen size to see how it adapts. You can see that in *Figure 14.15*.

Figure 14.15 – Style Book with a smaller view size

As shown in *Figure 14.15*, using the Style Book in this way as you go about making your own custom styles enables you to see changes and have control.

Styles offer a lot of opportunities; we've only discovered some basic flows in this chapter, but you should now have the foundations to start exploring yourself.

Summary

Styles opens up a world of styling opportunities for everyone. We've seen that by exploring some simple examples together. Let's recap what we have unlocked together:

- We learned what Styles are.

- We discovered how to use Styles and created a custom one.

- We learned how to add a custom Style to a block.

- We discovered what a Style Book is.

- We learned about multiple Styles and how to apply them to a theme.

Styling through Styles opens a world of possibilities. The editing interface is one you can trust for consistency – learn once and use it to create just what you want.

Now that we know how to use this, let's close out our journey of discovery together by looking at themes themselves, specifically block themes.

Question

Answer the following questions to test your knowledge of this chapter:

1. What is the Style Book?

   a. A way to view `theme.json`

   b. A way to view Styles across blocks

2. Multiple Style versions are possible and are called...?

   a. Style multiples

   b. Style variations

   c. Style duplicates

3. What file powers Styles?

   a. `Block.json`

   b. `Style.json`

   c. `Theme.json`

Answers

1. What is the Style Book?

    b. A way to view Styles across blocks

2. Multiple Style versions are possible and are called…?

    b. Style variations

3. What file powers Styles?

    c. `Theme.json`

15

Discovering WordPress Block Themes

Our last chapter took us on an adventure of discovering Styles and unlocking the power of styling across the site with a consistent interface. We are now getting close to the end of our journey together, and as we approach the end, we will turn to themes.

A theme wraps everything up that we've talked about so far:

- Styling for blocks
- Templates and template parts
- The style for an entire site

The idea of a theme is you can change it as easily as your clothing, such as changing from a dress in the summer to a coat in the winter.

Block themes are a great response to the problem of themes changing everything. A block theme by its nature is intended to solve many of the consistency issues that Classic themes posed. The term classic refers to themes that were before block themes. Block themes are designed to be complete and easy to change. To return to the clothing analogy – you can change themes as easily as you would change your clothing without impacting your data or having to learn a new interface.

For this to work, block themes also need to be consistent, have the same naming conventions, and use the native interfaces of blocks. That is a wider conversation outside the scope of this chapter, but it's worth considering that block themes are a first step in answering the problem around themes, not the ultimate answer.

In this chapter, we will answer the following questions:

- What is a block theme?
- How do you use a block theme?
- Where can you find block themes?

We will then close out with a summary of what block themes are and explore how inspiring they can be.

What is a block theme?

In simple terms, a block theme is simply a theme that is created using WordPress blocks. You edit this theme within the Site Editor. These types of themes have been supported since version 5.9.

It is worth stating that other names have been used for block themes, so you might find documentation about full site themes that refers to them as editor themes. A lot of these concepts were new, and as the language was forming, several different terms were used.

We used block themes when showing examples such as Twenty Twenty-Four and using features such as template parts. Typically, a block theme doesn't just come with Styles; it also has template parts and templates – all the full features unlocked within a Site Editor. They also come with patterns and, often, block style variations, unlocking all the new functionality within one theme.

In *Chapter 13*, we looked at the difference between themes. Let's recap why you'd want to use a block theme as a user:

- You can take advantage of the Style interface.

- You benefit from all built-in blocks.

- All parts of your site are editable without code.

- Block themes do turn on Site Editing as a feature, but you can control some of the features' visibility through the theme.

- Often, block themes come with multiple Styles, so you get more styling options built into one theme.

There are many more development benefits, but for now, let's stick to the user-facing ones, as those are of most interest to us.

How do you use a block theme?

Like other themes, you can activate and start using it. That's all there is to it. However, so far, we've jumped straight in using a theme already activated, so in this chapter, we are going to explore adding, finding, and searching for themes.

First, go to **Appearance** and then to **Themes**. Notice that I have **Twenty Twenty-Three** activated. You might have a different theme.

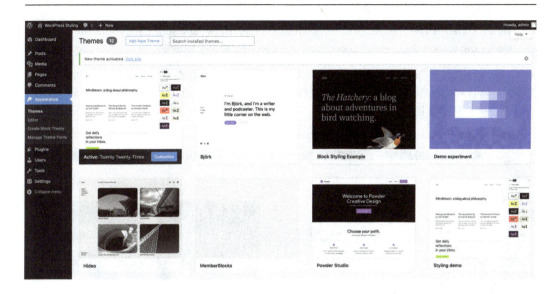

Figure 15.1 – The theme browser within WordPress

I am going to switch to using Twenty Twenty-Four, as it's been used so far in a lot of our examples. Before we do that, we might want to know a little more about it. So, hover over the image, and an option called Theme Details will appear. Let's click on that.

The next screenshot shows the modal that summarizes the theme.

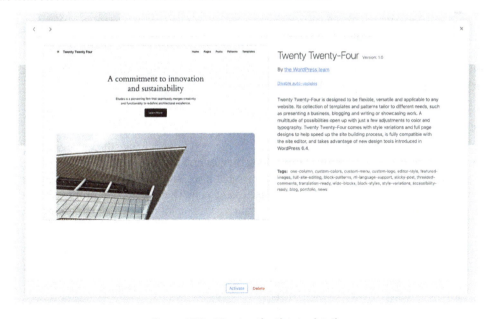

Figure 15.2 – Viewing the theme details

Once you click **Theme Details**, you will be taken to a screen showing a summary about the theme. This includes the author, tags, what version it is, and even the ability to delete or activate the theme.

In our case, we want to "activate" this theme to use it. Once you click **Activate**, you are taken back to the previous screen, and if successful, you should see a message saying **New theme activated**, alongside a link to view the site.

Figure 15.3 shows the theme activation message shown in the browser.

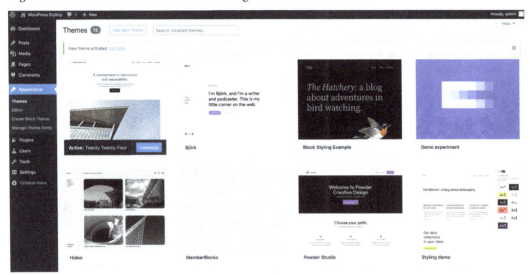

Figure 15.3 – New theme activated messaging

That really is all there is to viewing the theme and activating it. You can try out different themes using this method and see what they look like with your content.

> **Note**
>
> A word of caution though – when you change a theme, you might change the settings across your site. We have already discussed how block themes and the Site Editor functionality is designed to not cause issues when changing themes, but if you change from a non-block theme or possibly non-default theme, your experience might vary. There is work in progress at the time of writing to preserve changes globally, but there is still at lot that needs to be done here.

Let's now move on to where you can find block themes. By doing this, we will expand your options in discovering the perfect theme for your site.

Where can you find block themes?

We have looked a lot at default themes – that is, those that come with versions of WordPress. At the end of every year, a new default theme is released, and the past couple of years have seen options for block-related themes. This includes Twenty Twenty-Two, Twenty Twenty-Three, and the latest, Twenty Twenty-Four.

However, you might not want to use just those themes, and there are easy ways to find others.

Within WordPress, under **Themes**, there is the **Add themes** option. If you click that, a browsing interface opens. This is the same theme directory that you can reach online through `https://wordpress.org/themes/`, yet this can be accessed right there within the site itself (see *Figure 15.4*).

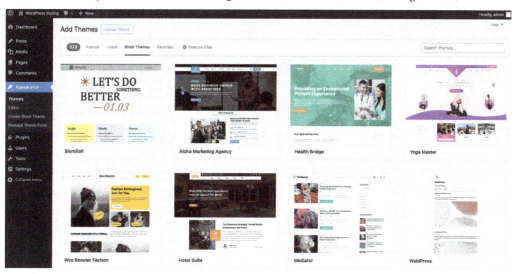

Figure 15.4 – Searching for block themes

In *Figure 15.4*, you can see that there is a section entitled **Block Themes**. This is helpful in surfacing themes that you know are going to optimize the Site Editor for you.

Once you click that, you will see the view change and load all the themes, which are block themes.

You can even search more in-depth by clicking **Feature Filter**, as shown in *Figure 15.5*.

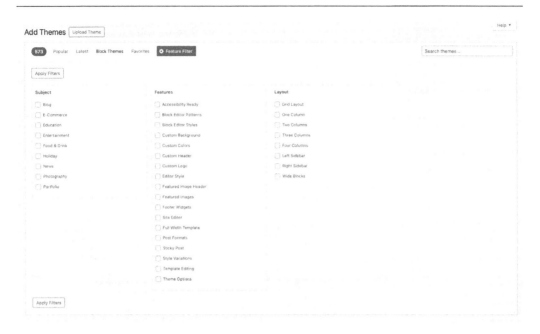

Figure 15.5 – Filtering themes in the search

Once you are in the filtering section, you can select any combination you want to really find that perfect fit. Under the **Features** column, select **Site Editor** to keep it filtered to these types of themes. You can also click **Block Themes** on the tab.

This is all great, but what about going even further and finding out more in-depth information about a theme before you try it? Downloading and trying each theme out on your site might be a laborious task. Sometimes, you want to just see something in a demo or find out more without adding it first.

You can do that within the WordPress theme directory. In the directory, you can easily search using the same criteria you would on the site, as shown in *Figure 15.6*.

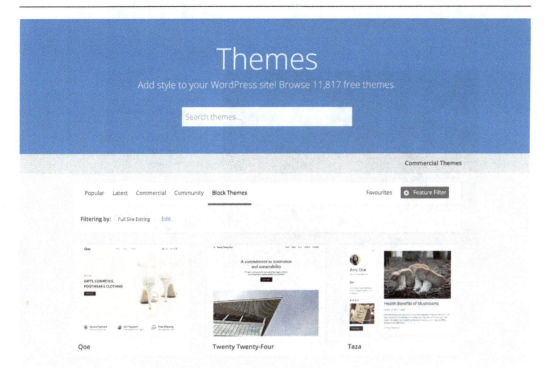

Figure 15.6 – Using the WordPress theme directory

Clicking **Block Themes** will load the themes of that type, and you can also save them under **Favourites** to build up a collection to return to.

It's worth noting there is also a link called **Commercial Themes** here. We talked about these types of themes before in *Chapter 13*. These themes have been curated as a recommended list by the theme review team within WordPress. If you are looking for a commercial theme, they are worth exploring. You might be looking for something a little extra you can't find for free, or perhaps you are looking for specific plugin support, such as a shop through WooCommerce. You can do that by picking a theme that has support for that plugin built into it.

The interface view for the theme within the theme directory is more expansive, giving you not only the option to preview but also download. In addition, it shows not only the Style variations and patterns but also important details, such as a **Support** link and statistics.

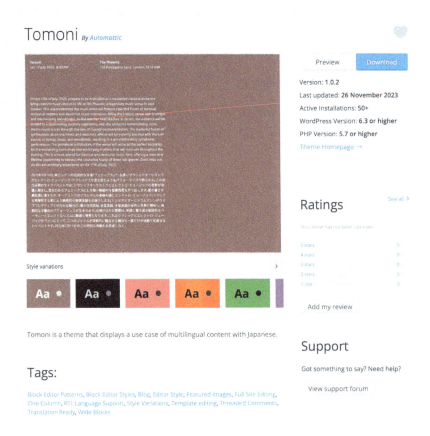

Figure 15.7 – A theme details view

The **Preview** option, as shown in *Figure 15.7*, allows you to explore test data to see what this theme might look like. This is a great way of browsing and discovering new themes. By exploring ratings and what people have said about the theme, you can learn what might work or might not for your site.

There are many other options to find themes you might want to try; a good one is following one of the amazing WordPress news and resources around the Site Editor and in general. A few of these include the following:

- **WP Tavern**: This can be found at `https://wptavern.com/`. It is a general theme news resource but often has theme-specific posts under `https://wptavern.com/category/themes`.

- **Gutenberg Times**: This resource has everything you ever wanted to know about the Site Editor and much more. It focuses on developer insights, and you can find theme-specific ones and even those just for patterns, templates, themes by selecting various filters under **News**: `https://gutenbergtimes.com/news/`.

We are now going to shift our attention to look at a great initiative, one that originated from the WordPress community. Often, groups come together to create themes, so let's look at one of those by exploring **community initiative themes**.

Community initiative themes

These are themes found under the **Community** filter in the WordPress theme directory. Themes such as Blue Note (`https://wordpress.org/themes/blue-note/`) are created by multiple people across the community coming together. You can discover more of these themes here: `https://wordpress.org/themes/browse/community/`. The Blue Note theme shown in *Figure 15.8* is high impact but simple in its layout. The images you use can stand out with strong, bold typography and expansive spacing.

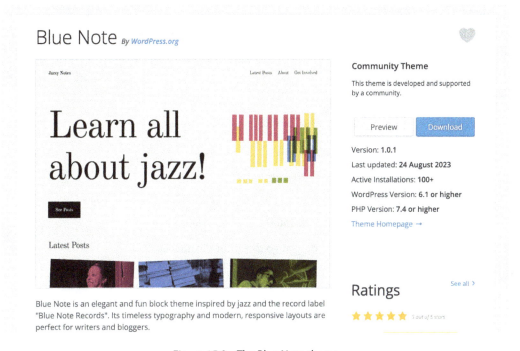

Figure 15.8 – The Blue Note theme

Block themes are incredible, and the different types of theme styles you can explore are numerous; there are more released each week. You can find just what you want for your site, and the process of finding a theme is half the fun.

Before we move on to the final chapter, we will now wrap up what we have learned in this chapter and close our journey into themes.

Summary

This journey into themes has taught us a lot. We now have not only a better understanding of themes and the context of where they have come from but also some specific knowledge of block themes and themes today. In this chapter, we covered the following together:

- We learned what block themes are.

- We discovered how to add and activate a block theme.

- We learned how to search and find block themes in the directory within our sites and in the WordPress theme directory.

- Together, we discovered other resources for themes.

Now, with this knowledge, let's bring our adventure to a close, thinking about where all this information leaves us. How have block themes inspired us? How can we start to create our own themes, and what is the next stage?

Questions

Answer the following questions to test your knowledge of this chapter:

1. What isn't a reason to use a block theme?

   a. It doesn't allow editing without knowing code.

   b. You get the same benefit from built-in blocks.

   c. You can take advantage of the Style interface.

2. To activate a block theme, where do you go to within the interface?

   a. **Customize | Themes**

   b. **Appearance | Themes**

   c. **Themes | Dashboard**

3. Where can you find block themes?

   a. Only in your WordPress installation under **Appearance | Themes | Add Themes**

   b. Only in the WordPress theme directory

   c. In both your WordPress installation under **Appearance | Themes | Add Themes** and the WordPress theme directory

Answers

1. What isn't a reason to use a block theme?

   a. It doesn't allow editing without knowing code.

2. To activate a block theme, where do you go to?

   b. **Appearance | Themes**

3. Where can you find block themes?

   c. In both your WordPress installation under **Appearance | Themes | Add Themes** and the WordPress Theme Directory

16

Wrapping Up Themes

In the previous chapters, we looked at the entire aspect of WordPress styling, as far as themes. It's been quite a journey, and we are going to close by looking at how inspiring block themes can be. We will also review resources for you to explore yourself as you develop your understanding of themes, along with sharing some theme resources.

In this book, we have covered a lot of topics. We began looking at blocks and then journeyed through design tools, looking at how those interacted with blocks. Our adventure took us to discovering patterns and the power they unlock. Then, we explored the site-editing experience together, unlocking template parts and templates. All of this built up to us being able to add styling to blocks, create our own patterns, and then modify existing themes. We've learned a lot, including a vast number of interfaces and new terminology related to styling WordPress.

In this chapter, we will explore the following topics:

- How block themes spark inspiration
- Themes that have additional functionality
- The Create Block Theme plugin
- Theme resources

We will then conclude this book and our discoveries with a final review of what we have discussed.

How block themes spark inspiration

Nowadays, there is a lot of inspiration to be found in themes. This statement might seem bold, but it is true. In the past, themes felt very much the same. Block themes open up a world of possibilities and often enable you to do things previously not possible with themes alone. For example, because block themes come with multiple patterns, you can swap in other patterns and still maintain their preset styles. You can also select from tailored styles that instantly change an entire site. In the earlier version of WordPress, using the non-block-based editor, you would have to use a theme framework or know extensive custom CSS to achieve this.

Let's take a look at Twenty Twenty-Four, the latest default theme, to learn a bit more about it and take some inspiration from that understanding.

Initially, when you look at it, you just see the base theme, but you get a lot more besides. You get a vast range of patterns, as shown in the following figure.

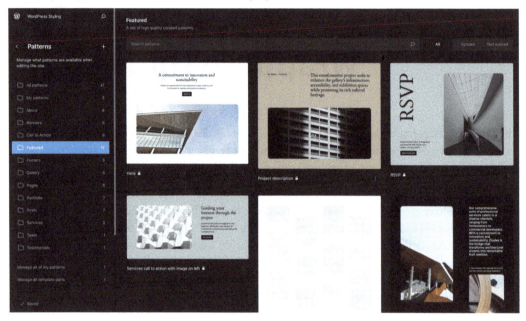

Figure 16.1 – Patterns in the default theme

You get a lot packaged into each theme, template parts, patterns, and styling, which is why looking for inspiration within default themes each year is a great idea. You can start doing this by checking out the theme demo sites, example such as `https://2024.wordpress.net/`. You can also explore a preview of the Twenty Twenty-Four theme here:

Learn from the previous default themes

One of the big things you can do is learn from the older default themes. As mentioned before, perhaps one of the biggest lessons you can do each year when a new theme is released is to not only explore that but also compare it with previous ones.

In order to explore some of those older ones, you can both view them on your WordPress site and explore their demo sites. Here are the block theme-specific ones:

- **Twenty Twenty-Three**: `https://2023.wordpress.net/`
- **Twenty Twenty-Two**: `https://2022.wordpress.net/`

As you can see, block themes are incredibly inspiring, and looking at the default themes released each year is a great start. However, there might be something you want to achieve that goes a bit further. Let's look next at themes that do specific functionality, which was previously challenging to achieve.

Themes that have additional functionality

It is worthwhile looking at the theme directory as the next destination after default themes. The WordPress theme directory is a shared and curated place that you can explore by filtering. Let's have a look at some themes that unlock functionality, which, before block themes and the Site Editor, was previously hard to achieve without a plugin or extensive code knowledge.

Moog

This theme was created by Elma Studio and is incredible; it can be found at `https://wordpress.org/themes/moog/`. You can see the demo image on the theme site, as shown in *Figure 16.2*.

Figure 16.2 – A website using the Moog theme with demo content

The reason I wanted to use this as an example is its grid layout. Often, creating these types of layouts in a grid was challenging in the past. It's worth noting that a lot of what previously was a problem to achieve is now a thing of the past thanks to the power of block themes.

Oaknut

This theme by Anders Norén is a visual delight and solves the problem of a Linktree-esque layout, which is a layout that shows a list of social, personal, or business links. While this might seem to be a small issue, it's actually one that a WordPress site can effectively solve, either in isolation of combined with other pages. You can find the site here: `https://wordpress.org/themes/oaknut/`.

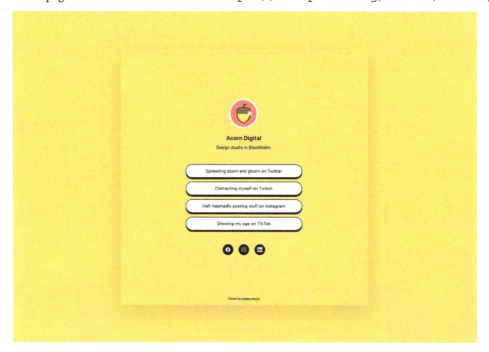

Figure 16.3 – A website using the Oaknut theme with demo content

This theme comes with 23 built in styles, lots of fonts, and everything you need to create this layout.

Moving on from these unique layouts, one of the issues of the past was limited styling or having to use a framework. That's where the new multiple patterns and themes come in, which have companion plugins.

Powder Studio

This theme by Brian Gardner can be found here: `https://wordpress.org/themes/powder/`. This is a theme that sets out to have a foundation you can build from, rather than just being aimed at a specific type. Sometimes, it is nice to simply solve one problem, while at other times, you might want to a theme foundation and adapt it to suit your needs, or integrate it into your site. That's where themes like these come into their own.

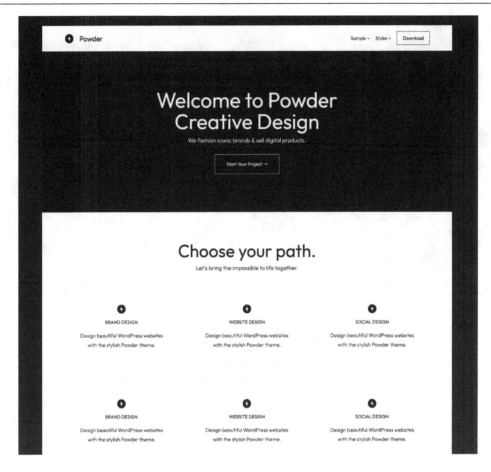

Figure 16.4 – A website using Powder with demo content

By combining the styles, patterns and templates this theme comes with you can create from a small starting point or dive right in.

Ollie

Ollie is a theme by Mike McAlister and Patrick Posner. This theme can be found here: `https://wordpress.org/themes/ollie/`. This theme, which can be seen in *Figure 16.5*, looks deceptively simple but is much more powerful in what it can do. Just like Powder, this has a range of elements that can be combined to create an almost endless combination of sites.

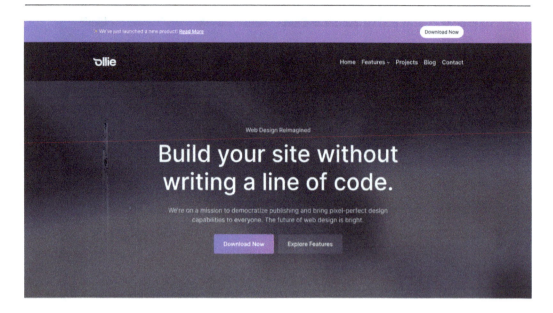

Figure 16.5 – A website using the Ollie theme with demo content

This theme has so many patterns, templates and parts (along with styles) that you can truly create just what you want. It also has some incredible guidance along the way. Themes such as this really help unlock your capabilities in discovering and exploring possible combinations.

> **Note**
>
> Don't forget when you are trying out a new theme to always try the demo sites. They will tell you what each theme creator thinks can be created.

As we conclude this section with these few examples, it's worth saying these are just from the theme directory within WordPress. I haven't touched on commercial themes or ones that might do specific things, such as work optimized with a plugin such as WooCommerce. There is a whole world of themes and possibilities that can be unlocked with block themes.

We've seen a few themes that bring additional functions that weren't possible or were difficult before block themes. Let's move on and explore how we can start to create our own block themes using a helpful plugin.

The Create Block Theme plugin

In *Chapter 3*, we looked briefly at cloning Twenty Twenty-Three using this plugin. There are, however, more settings you can do with this, so it's worth exploring a bit more as we are now further into the journey.

While having an existing theme is great, you might want to go further as you progress in your journey, or you might even have a template to create your own. That's what this plugin allows you to do.

To recap, you can get this plugin from the WordPress plugin directory at `https://wordpress.org/plugins/create-block-theme/`, or you can get it from within your installation. Let's activate it and see what we can do with it now.

Just like when we used the other default theme, you need to ensure you have activated the theme you want to create from first. In our case, make sure you have the theme Twenty Twenty-Four activated.

Now, we are going to search for **Create Block Theme** and click **Install Now**. Then, you want to click **Activate** again. You can see this in *Figure 16.6*. If you have this installed from the previous example you don't need to do it again.

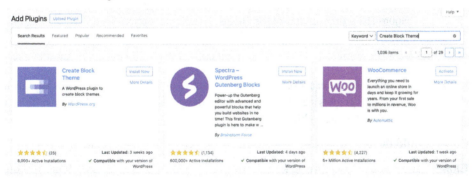

Figure 16.6 – Searching for create block on the Add Plugins screen in WordPress

By following these steps, you add the plugin.

Let's discover how to do this in the following figure, where we go to **Appearance** and then **Create Block Theme** to see the export settings. By exporting, we create the theme we want.

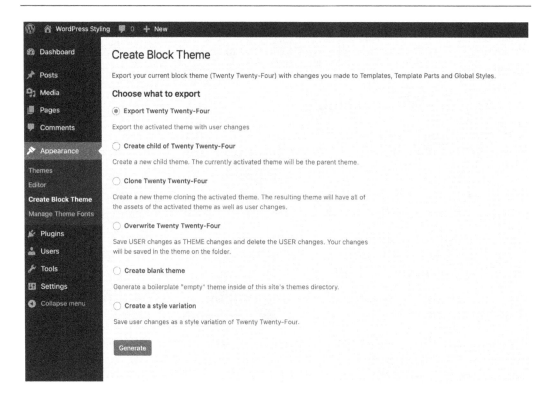

Figure 16.7 – An overview of the Create Block Theme options page

All those settings are quite numerous; let's walk through each of the following and what they mean:

- **Export theme**: This takes an exact version of what is active on the site. This includes any custom changes or Styles. This creates a ZIP file that will be downloaded, just like the next options we are going to look at – "create a child" and "clone."

- **Create a child theme**: This creates one based on the currently active theme.

- **Clone**: This takes the same theme and allows you to make changes in that clone. You don't want to edit core or theme default files, as this might cause issues when you update themes or WordPress, with your changes being overwritten.

- **Overwrite theme**: Ideally, you don't want to do this with default themes, as it saves user settings as theme ones. If the default theme gets updated, changes that were made with this option would be overwritten and gone for good. This option is ideal if you work on a custom theme and are never going to update from a source, but it's not if you are using a purchased or default theme.

- **Create blank theme**: This is useful if you are creating a new theme and want a foundation base.

- **Create a style variation**: This is another great option as you learn to create themes and Styles. Here, you can save any customizations as a Style variation. It is worth noting that this behaves similar to "Overwrite theme." If this gets updated, the files are removed, and the entire theme directory is replaced with the update.

For our demo, we are going to create a block theme to have an empty one to work from (see *Figure 16.8*).

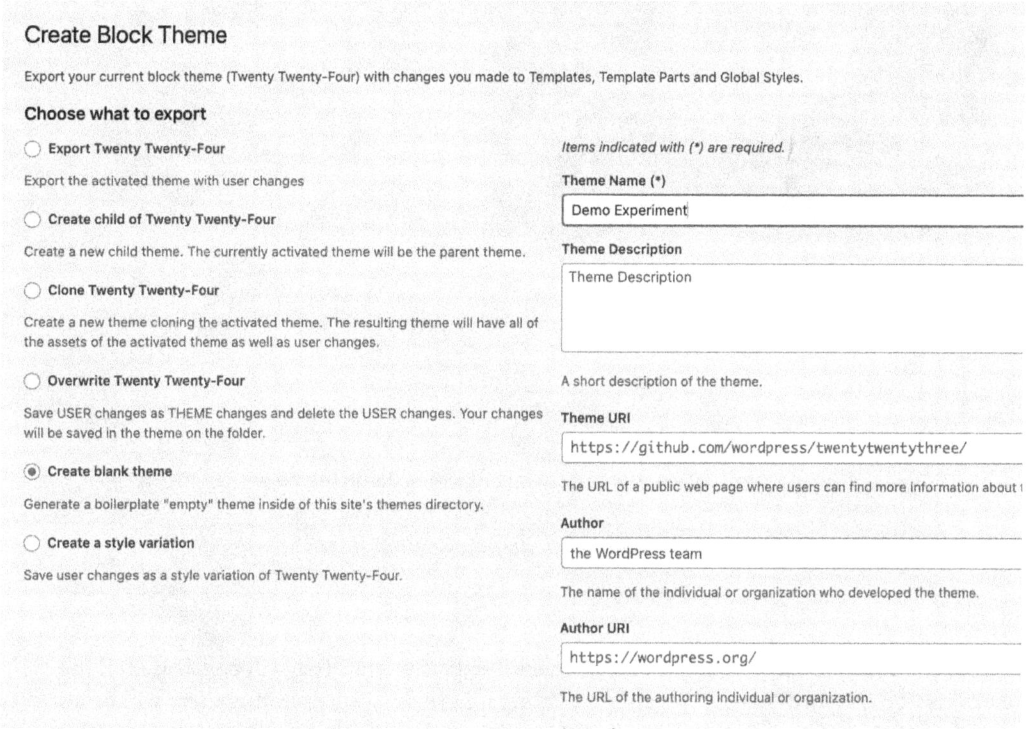

Figure 16.8 – The Create Blank Theme option selected, showing the fields to edit

Once you select all the fields that must be filled out, you can move on to creating the theme. That's all you need to do to create an empty theme – cool, right? If you view this theme, you can see that it's already in the theme browser for you.

Let's see how the modal now looks when we view the theme we have created, as shown in *Figure 16.9*.

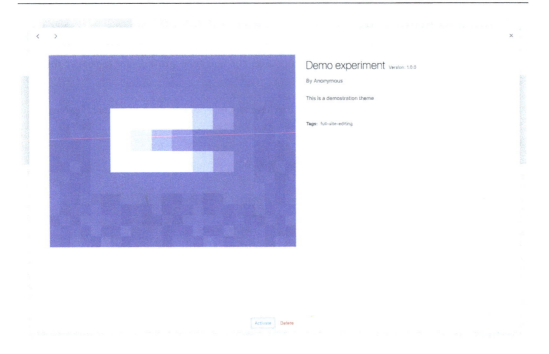

Figure 16.9 – A theme details card with a demo theme

We can then do a range of things to explore more themes.

> **Note**
> At the time of writing, theme font management is experimental. This will be released in the next version of WordPress, so we aren't covering it here. It is worth noting there will be an interface to manage this, available for everyone, expected to be released with WordPress 6.5.

The theme we have created has the basics and template files you may require but no styles.

Our attention will now turn to considering how we can add to our knowledge, by looking at and following some theme-related resources. We've already learned why block themes are useful, how they work, and even how to create a simple one for ourselves. Let's go further by seeing how we can expand our knowledge.

Theme resources

We have already shared a lot of resources, but in the final chapter, it's worth concluding with some further examples. So, let's do just that.

If you want your journey to go even further, there is the `WordPress.org` theme team: `https://make.wordpress.org/themes/` While this is a team for contribution, it also often has information about themes and insights, so it's worth mentioning here for those that want to continue their journey, start learning about contributing to the project, and even start to review themes themselves, while learning how to create themes as they do so.

If you want to learn more, here are some useful links related to creating themes:

- **WordPress Developer Blog – the Themes section**: `https://developer.wordpress.org/news/category/themes/`. This resource is the official developer blog and has a section just for theme news and information.
- **The WordPress theme handbook**: `https://developer.wordpress.org/themes/`. This is a place to learn and discover guidelines related to creating themes.
- **WordPress free theme courses**: `https://learn.wordpress.org/?s=themes`. This is a free community maintained resource relating to themes.

As a last piece of advice, when you are creating a theme, think about its format. As we mentioned in previous chapters, embrace sketching it out. Think about how it could look. Look and save sites for inspiration, and think about taking inspiration beyond websites, like we considered for patterns. When you are looking at the theme, also look at what you are trying to create fits into the market. What are others doing in that space, and how are they achieving it with their site?

There is a lot to discover once you start creating your own themes; adjusting styling is just the start. It's most likely as you explore the layers build up naturally and you discover the concepts through adjusting using Styles, then creating a pattern, to eventually creating your own template parts, and even a theme. The key is to have fun and enjoy using all these new features as you explore.

Summary

We have learned quite a bit together, starting with blocks and concluding with themes in this chapter. Our journey has taught us a lot of new languages, and we've learned how to create sites and layouts that were previously only possible with experienced CSS, unlocking some powerful styling.

In this chapter, we achieved the following:

- We learned how and why block themes can inspire.
- We discovered that default themes are a great starting point and a source of inspiration, also through their demos.

- We explored some themes that can do things that were complicated before block themes.

- We learned about the Create Block Theme plugin and how to use it.

- We discovered some theme resources and options to go even further in our theme journey.

It's been a lot to cover, and I hope you've enjoyed this start to your discovery of blocks, patterns, templates, styles, and themes. This is just the beginning – there is so much more you can start to explore now. Perhaps you will even begin to create your own theme one day. You can start simply, just changing the style of a block, and then, as you grow in confidence, explore even more.

In your journey, don't forget there are many resources out there and lots of incredible themes to use to boost your creations. Take your time and enjoy your discovery as you grow in confidence, using design tools and the power of the WordPress editing experience.

Don't forget to share what you create; maybe it's a pattern you send to the pattern directory of WordPress, or even just something you share with a friend. Pass on the knowledge you've gained. Look for inspiration on other sites as you also grow in confidence. Start considering how you can use the tools and things WordPress has in different ways. Above all, have fun, experiment, and don't forget – you can always use the undo option.

Questions

Answer the following questions to test your knowledge of this chapter:

1. The name of the team of contributors that review themes for the WordPress theme directory are called what?

    a. The WordPress theme review team

    b. The reviewers

2. Which of the following is a list of default block themes?

    a. Cloud, Rain, and Twenty-Twenty-Four

    b. Twenty Eighteen and Twenty-Twenty

    c. Twenty Twenty-Two, Twenty Twenty-Three, and Twenty Twenty-Four

3. What is the Create Block Theme plugin?

    a. A plugin you can use to create block themes

    b. A plugin you can use to create blocks and theme templates

Answers

1. The name of the team of contributors that review themes for the WordPress theme directory are called what?

    a. The WordPress theme review team

2. Which of the following is a list of default block themes?

    c. Twenty Twenty-Two, Twenty Twenty-Three, and Twenty Twenty-Four

3. What is the Create Block Theme plugin?

    a. A plugin you can use to create block themes

Index

packtpub.com

Subscribe to our online digital library for full access to over 7,000 books and videos, as well as industry leading tools to help you plan your personal development and advance your career. For more information, please visit our website.

Why subscribe?

- Spend less time learning and more time coding with practical eBooks and Videos from over 4,000 industry professionals

- Improve your learning with Skill Plans built especially for you

- Get a free eBook or video every month

- Fully searchable for easy access to vital information

- Copy and paste, print, and bookmark content

Did you know that Packt offers eBook versions of every book published, with PDF and ePub files available? You can upgrade to the eBook version at packtpub.com and as a print book customer, you are entitled to a discount on the eBook copy. Get in touch with us at customercare@packtpub.com for more details.

At www.packtpub.com, you can also read a collection of free technical articles, sign up for a range of free newsletters, and receive exclusive discounts and offers on Packt books and eBooks.

A Book That You May Enjoy

If you enjoyed this book, you may be interested in this other book by Packt:

WordPress Plugin Development Cookbook

Yannick Lefebvre

ISBN: 978-1-80181-077-7

- Discover action and filter hooks, which form the basis of plugin creation
- Explore the creation of administration pages and add new content management sections through custom post types and custom fields
- Add new components to the block editor library
- Fetch, cache, and regularly update data from external sources
- Bring in external data sources to enhance your content
- Make your pages dynamic by using JavaScript, jQuery, and AJAX and adding new widgets to the platform
- Add support for plugin translation and distributing your work to the WordPress community

Packt is searching for authors like you

If you're interested in becoming an author for Packt, please visit authors.packtpub.com and apply today. We have worked with thousands of developers and tech professionals, just like you, to help them share their insight with the global tech community. You can make a general application, apply for a specific hot topic that we are recruiting an author for, or submit your own idea.

Share Your Thoughts

Now you've finished *WordPress styling with blocks, patterns, templates and themes*, we'd love to hear your thoughts! Scan the QR code below to go straight to the Amazon review page for this book and share your feedback or leave a review on the site that you purchased it from.

https://packt.link/r/1804618500

Your review is important to us and the tech community and will help us make sure we're delivering excellent quality content.

Download a free PDF copy of this book

Thanks for purchasing this book!

Do you like to read on the go but are unable to carry your print books everywhere?

Is your eBook purchase not compatible with the device of your choice?

Don't worry, now with every Packt book you get a DRM-free PDF version of that book at no cost.

Read anywhere, any place, on any device. Search, copy, and paste code from your favorite technical books directly into your application.

The perks don't stop there, you can get exclusive access to discounts, newsletters, and great free content in your inbox daily

Follow these simple steps to get the benefits:

1. Scan the QR code or visit the link below

https://packt.link/free-ebook/9781804618509

2. Submit your proof of purchase

3. That's it! We'll send your free PDF and other benefits to your email directly

www.ingramcontent.com/pod-product-compliance
Lightning Source LLC
Chambersburg PA
CBHW080633060326
40690CB00021B/4918